FAITH IN A
RISK-TAKING GOD

FAITH IN A
RISK-TAKING GOD

Edward Patey

DARTON, LONGMAN AND TODD
LONDON

First published in 1991 by
Darton, Longman and Todd Ltd
89 Lillie Road, London SW6 1UD

© 1991 Edward Patey

ISBN 0–232–51936–6

A catalogue record for this book is available
from the British Library

Phototypeset by Intype, London
Printed and bound in Great Britain
Courier International Ltd, East Kilbride

We must recognise soberly that no planning
of the Church's future in the next decades
can relieve us of the necessity of going
forward into a future that cannot be
planned, of risk, of danger, and of hope
in the incalculable grace of God.

Karl Rahner sj

CONTENTS

ACKNOWLEDGEMENTS

FEW BOOKS published during the second half of the twentieth century so profoundly influenced my understanding of the Church and its prospects for the future as Karl Rahner's *The Shape of the Church to Come*. It was published in an English edition (translated by Edward Quinn) in 1974. It is now out of print. I am grateful to the publishers, SPCK, for allowing me to include a number of extracts in this book. Those familiar with Karl Rahner will recognise his prophetic influence in the following pages even in passages where he is not directly quoted.

I have made considerable use of two episcopal reports which aroused much critical interest. *The Nature of Christian Belief* is a statement and exposition by the House of Bishops of the General Synod of the Church of England (Church House Publishing 1986). *The Easter People* is a message by the Roman Catholic Bishops of England and Wales in response to the Liverpool Pastoral Congress (St Paul Publications, Slough 1980). I am grateful to the publishers of these two significant reports for permission to quote extracts.

The weekly journal *The Tablet* provides a regular fare of comment and criticism on theological, ecclesiastical, political and other matters of Christian concern. I am grateful for permission to include a number of extracts from articles and correspondence which first appeared in its pages.

The ideas which are set out in this book have developed in the author's mind over many years and have their origin in books and journals read, conferences attended, lectures and sermons heard and innumerable conversations with friends and colleagues. Wherever possible sources are given and acknowledged in the notes. I offer my thanks to all who have knowingly or unknowingly contributed to the pages which follow. I apologise to any who find that they have been misinterpreted by being quoted out of context.

Bible quotations are from the Jerusalem Bible, published and copyright 1966, 1967 and 1968 by Darton, Longman and Todd Ltd and Doubleday & Co Inc, and used by permission of the publishers.

E.H.P.

1

PRESENT INDICATIVES

IN THE CLOSING MONTHS of 1990 it seemed as though the Churches in England were beginning to look towards the future with a renewal of hope. The announcement that Dr George Carey was to succeed Dr Robert Runcie as Archbishop of Canterbury provided one reason for this new-found optimism. After the undignified hype in the media and among the bookmakers, the appointment of a comparatively young and unknown bishop to the Anglican top job appeared to many to herald a new look in the upper leadership of the Church. Newspaper comment suggested that here was a new broom who would give a much needed spring clean to the Established Church. Some of Dr Carey's early remarks encouraged that belief. Three months later a series of important ceremonies heralded a new determination on the part of the Churches in Britain to move forward together on an ecumenical pilgrimage which committed them to find ways of achieving greater unity. Early in 1991, on the original initiative of Pope John Paul II, and with the strong support of the Anglican bishops and other leaders, a Decade of Evangelism was announced, to which the new archbishop pledged his wholehearted support. Do these activities herald a breakaway from old leadership styles, a fresh ecumenical commitment after the failure of so many earlier schemes, and an undertaking on the part of the Churches to be less concerned with the preservation of their own traditional structures in order to give greater priority to the needs of the vast majority of men and women in the land for whom the Church and its message appear irrelevant? If the final years of the twentieth century see the Church fixing its eyes on the future in the spirit of renewal, this can give cause for modest optimism.

But such ecclesiastical euphoria must not be allowed to obscure the fact that neither a new archbishop, nor a fresh ecumenical undertaking, nor a nation-wide evangelistic enterprise, can relieve us of the task of continuing to face up to all those areas of disagreement among Christians which have occupied so much ecclesiastical time and consumed so many tonnes of paper in recent years. None of the great questions of belief and action which confront us can be solved at a stroke, nor is it desirable that they should be. Christian faith is an invitation to continuous exploration, not to quick-fire pre-packaged solutions.

If the Church of England decides within the next year or so to ordain women to the priesthood, it will not remove the anxiety felt by many Anglicans, nor make relations with the Roman Catholic Church any easier. If new leadership encourages a return to traditional reliance on the absolute authority of Scripture and the historic creeds as the only basis for Christian life and witness, this will not prevent an increasing number of thoughtful people becoming convinced that much orthodox biblical and doctrinal teaching is no longer entirely compatible with honest scholarship and modern scientific discovery. If the decade of evangelism leads to a proliferation of Billy Graham type campaigns and fundamentalist 'happenings', others will question the efficacy of missions of this kind, and would press for a more radical and prophetic Christian involvement in political, economic, cultural and social affairs. New ecumenical structures will be subjected to critical scrutiny by those who have seen so many previous schemes come to grief. Others, looking at the agendas of synods and Church committees will ask whether the Church's concern for its own internal health prevents it from taking seriously the world it is supposed to be serving. It will be further asked whether the Church can serve that world effectively with its out-of-date machinery. Can traditional patterns of ministry and parochial strategy be expected to work efficiently in our multi-cultural and highly mobile society?

When people discuss their hopes for the future of the Church and its mission there are always demands that those in authority should 'give a lead'. When this is said it generally means that people are asking that their own prejudices and preferences should be ratified from on high. People have every right to hold their own strong opinions and to try to persuade others to agree with them. But neither new leaders nor synodical resolutions nor ecclesiastical reports can force Christians to agree precisely on all the major areas of theological or ecclesiastical debate on which opinions are clearly divided. These divisions occur among people of equal integrity, intelligence and spirituality, and with equal access to the Holy Scriptures and doctrines of the Church. Official statements and resolutions are issued with the intention of papering over the cracks, but the cracks remain. To pretend that they do not exist is ultimately to weaken the Christian witness. There is no absolute infallibility. To pretend otherwise is folly.

There are many lessons to be learned from what are now being dubbed 'the Runcie years', and they are worth pondering over with an eye to the future. When Robert Runcie announced his retirement from the see of Canterbury, the gentlemen and ladies of the press were less than generous about him. He had for long been a soft target for the cartoonists, satirists and the makers of Spitting Image. He had already been described as a spiritual leader who 'always nailed his colours to the fence'. John Harriott wrote bitterly of the 'tabloid rottweilers who had been hungry for Runcie's blood precisely because he would not endorse their own rotten values'. With the appointment of his successor a writer in the *Observer* said, 'Dr Runcie leaves behind him a legacy of unresolved problems and old conflicts within the Church.' At the same time, Dr William Oddie (who has since become a Roman Catholic) contributed an article to a newspaper with the caption 'Canterbury goes Christian'.

During his ten years at Lambeth Dr Runcie had to face no shortage of tough problems. There was the long-running debate about the ordination of women. The problems of homosexual relations and, in particular, of 'gay' clergy demanded his urgent attention. Church unity questions, particularly between the Anglican and Roman Catholic Churches, were continually on his agenda. He had to preside over difficult discussion on divisive theological issues raised by Bishop Jenkins of Durham and others. There were complex ethical and political questions to be dealt with, such as the nature of the Thanksgiving Service following the Falklands war, and his determination that an act of solemn worship should not be the occasion for jingoism or triumphalism. Hostilities in the Gulf broke out a few weeks before his retirement, demanding appropriate archiepiscopal comment. The report of his commission on urban priority areas, *Faith in the City*, brought him into conflict with the Government who disliked what seemed to be criticism of Margaret Thatcher's monetarist policy. A later report, *Faith in the Countryside*, was leaked just before publication and gave the press the opportunity of anticipating another clash between Lambeth Palace and Downing Street, assuming that it was certain to infuriate the Prime Minister. The newspapers made what mileage they could out of the apparent tension between the spiritual and political leaders, living so close to one another on either side of the Thames.

Together with the burden of the archbishop's job at a time of great change in Church and state, Runcie had grievous personal burdens to bear: his daily anxiety over the fate of his personal representative Terry Waite, taken hostage in Lebanon, and the tragic affair of the Crockford Preface, and the suicide of Dr Gareth Bennett. Few archbishops of Canterbury have had so many difficult and controversial questions to face, and in every instance he was beset by pressure groups and one-track-mind factions intent on soliciting support for their own particular points of view. If he failed they would complain bitterly of his lack of leadership. But Runcie had no natural taste for polemics. He once said, 'I am the archbishop of a Church in which the tension between orthodoxy and liberalism remains unresolved. I cannot claim to be above these tensions. They run right through me.' His biographer, Adrian Hastings,[1] summed up his character: 'He is incapable of not seeing both sides of every question. He never finds it easy to know which side to back, though he has in the end managed to do this more often than his critics like to admit.' Some critics, hopeful of a future for the Church of England under a new archbishop, have almost hinted that Runcie himself was a major cause of the troubles which beset the Church during the 1980s. Runcie himself said that all he was trying to do was 'to prevent the Church of England from trying to sting itself to death like a demented scorpion'.

The appointment of Dr George Carey as Runcie's successor

came as a surprise to everyone including, apparently, the man himself. Clifford Longley, in *The Times*, hailed it as an exciting appointment, bold and even risky. 'One of the youngest and most junior bishops has leap-frogged the entire roomful of his elders and betters. It provided,' he said, 'a chance, perhaps a last chance, for the Church of England to do something different and thereby break out of its gentle downward slope.' The popular press relished the news that here was a man who had left school at fifteen with no qualifications, thus breaking the Lambeth-Oxbridge mould; that he was a man of simple faith, converted by the warmth of evangelical fellowship, and a lover of the Bible. John Selwyn Gummer, Government minister and member of the Church of England General Synod, was quick to express his relief that 'here was a man whose view of the Christian faith has not been diminished by the theological minimalism now distorted by fashion-conscious liberals' – a scarcely veiled reference to the retiring archbishop. John Gummer's conservatism is faithfully reflected in his theological outlook. Much of the criticism of Robert Runcie's leadership style came from politicians whose instinct for self-preservation compelled them to adhere closely (at least in public) to the orthodoxy of the party line. They preferred the clarity of cut-and-dried statements which bore no risk of compromise. The Church has no party policy, only the commitment to explore the Christian message and to take sides with all who seek the coming of the kingdom of God, whatever their religious or political affiliation. Some politicians would like the bishops to act as parliamentary whips, but that cannot be their function. In the search for the deepest truths, pluralism is the name of the game. In the search for unity, love is the over-riding incentive.

Dr Carey, an experienced priest and competent theologian, must have found himself embarrassed by this 'simple gospel' image which was being foisted on him. He took the opportunity of his farewell address in his former cathedral of Wells to warn his congregation, and the nation at large, against what he described as the danger of simplism – 'that if only we can get back to the old, old story and away from dangerous theological thinking, then God will bless his people and all will be well. I can assure you that an emphasis on the essential verities of our faith does not mean a return to fundamentalism. God's truth is too profound, too wonderful for that. True evangelism does not avoid tough and sometimes embarrassing questions.'

Dr Carey illustrated his own ability to raise embarrassing questions when in a *Readers Digest* interview only a few weeks before his enthronement in Canterbury he said: 'The idea that only a male can represent Christ at the altar is a most serious heresy. The implications of that are devastating and destructive because it means that women feel totally excluded.' The storm of criticism which greeted these remarks, especially from those opposed to the ordination of women, was probably a painful reminder to him of the vulnerability facing him as Primate of All England. The apology in which he said that he regretted speaking of heresy rather than of theological error revealed a man strong enough to stick to his opinions in face of criticism. Theological error is only a slightly more polite way of saying heresy – it means much the same thing.

Dr Runcie summed up his own philosophy in a farewell message to the General Synod:

> Where this Synod has sometimes failed is in recognising the complexity of the world around or in thinking that a resolution passed will eliminate that complexity altogether. And there has sometimes seemed to be a panic that the Church will cease to exist if we do not do or say something now. There will never be uniformity. Conflict is inevitable. Truth is paramount. But to recognise goodness or some-times sanity in those with whom we are in frequent and fundamental disagreement, this is an Anglican grace which must not be lost.

Nor should it be only an Anglican grace. Christians of every tradition need to see the disagreements and difficulties which divide them not as disasters to be deplored but as the necessary ingredients for those pilgrim people of God who dare to have their eyes fixed firmly on the unknown future rather than on the familiar past where they like to feel at home.

The new Chief Rabbi, Dr Jonathan Sacks, discussed this same theme in the course of his 1991 Reith lectures for the BBC. 'Pluralism', he said, 'gives rise to deep and intractable conflicts while at the same time undermining the principles by which they might be resolved. It disintegrates our concept of the common good. It endorses mutually exclusive visions of the good and by abandoning the concept of a common good leaves us inarticulate in the face of cultural collision. From this deadlock there is a way out. And that is to think of a plural society not as one in which there is a babel of conflicting languages, but rather as one in which we each have to be bilingual.'

We must learn to see that pluralism, with all its attendant dangers, risks and mistakes, is the acceptance of the invitation of God to explore into the unknown in order to discover greater truths than we have yet been able to grasp. Both the Bible and science witness to the fact that honest exploration is the only way forward. Necessary ingredients for faith must include conflict, contradiction and uncomfortable compromise. Faith is a risky business.

So the way forward can only be achieved if the various parties, theologies, churchmanships, and pressure groups which make up today's Church can discover how to listen seriously and speak honestly to one another in that spirit of mutual love and concern for the common good which is to be expected of the followers of Jesus Christ. At the inaugural assembly of the World Council of Churches meeting in Amsterdam in 1948, those present issued a message in which they described their new-found ecumenical experience:

> As we have talked to each other here, we have begun to understand how our separation has prevented us from receiving correction from one another in Christ. And because we lacked this correction, the world has often heard from us not the word of God, but the words of men.

If the Churches, with all their continuing problems and deep differences of understanding, can move into the twenty-first century in this creative and dynamic spirit, compromise will no longer be a suspect word, but a sign of growing maturity in Christ – an edging towards the profounder truths which none of us has yet grasped. The gospel offers hope for the future, but only if we recognise that none of the questions which have worried us and divided us in the past will vanish overnight. We still have to go on wrestling with such questions as the ordination of women as priests and bishops. We still have to ask profound questions arising out of the shortage of ministers, which means for the Roman Catholics whether they should now allow their priests to be married and for Anglicans whether it might be right for certain lay women and men to celebrate the Holy Communion. And still the answers to such problems as embryo research, or nuclear power, or homosexual relations, will not be any easier for us in the next decade than they were in the past. Nor will the theological and biblical questions about the virginal conception of Jesus and his bodily resurrection, or the involvement of the Church in political and social affairs – these are things with which we shall have to go on living, and about which we shall have to continue to disagree. It is no good thinking, as some people hopefully do, that solutions will be any easier now that Archbishop Runcie has left Lambeth and Dr Leonard has left London, or even if David Jenkins should leave Durham! Even if one set of questions is successfully answered, another set, equally problematical, will be there to take its place.

It was not long before his untimely death at the end of 1990 that the brilliant Roman Catholic journalist, John Harriott, wrote in *The Tablet*:[2]

> Churchmen seduced into offering an easy fix are simply storing up future trouble. It has been one of Archbishop Runcie's strengths to recognise that danger and to try to create space and time for truth to emerge. This is no time for a Mickey Mouse Christianity.

When people started writing to the journal to ask what he meant by Mickey Mouse Christianity, John Harriott wrote a second piece in which he said:

> It needs to be said over and over again that Christianity is not a simple religion and cannot be reduced to simplistic terms. Christianity is not for buttonhole badges, sandwich boards, advertising slogans and wayside pulpits. The temptation to reduce Christianity to Christmas cracker phrases is often well intentioned but we should not be surprised if it ends in provoking uneasiness and contempt. The temptation to offer processed food – slick answers, easy sentimentalities, slogans and jingles – as representing the mind

and heart of Almighty God and the awesome mysteries of salvation may be powerful to an increasingly shallow culture, but there comes a point where even the laziest consumers begin to realise that it damages the health. Better for people to shrink from the gospel because it is too great than because it is too small.[3]

That is a timely warning as we face fresh opportunities for leadership, for ecumenism and for evangelism. Each of these initiatives holds out the possibilities of opening up new and challenging paths for the Churches to follow. But wherever they lead us, we shall easily go astray unless all our endeavours are undergirded by profound, honest and courageous study of our faith and life as followers of Jesus Christ, and in the context not of an age which is passing, but in terms of the scientific, cultural and social life of our own time and of the future. And this kind of theological and biblical study cannot be left in the hands of ecclesiastical professionals alone. It must involve lay women and men. It must also involve that wider constituency of people who we might call Christian fellow-travellers – those who are put off by what they see as the trivialities of the institutional Churches, but who are desperately searching for that understanding of life's meaning which we call the kingdom of God, and who sometimes seem to be nearer to it than those of us who are fully paid-up members.

This book argues neither for a clinging to the old ways nor for a negative truce between the various theological and ecclesiastical factions. That only leads to stalemate. If acceptance of one another is one mark of the unity of the Church, impatience with one another and with ourselves is another. Impatience, arising out of our readiness both to search for the truth and to love one another in Christian fellowship, must drive us relentlessly to make something positive and creative out of our divisions. This means that we must take great risks together, which Christians are usually remarkably unwilling to do. But the God of the Bible is not a play-safe God. At every point he reveals himself as a risk-taker. Nor is his Church called to play safe. It is to be a movement of men and women committed to explore the yet undiscovered purposes of God for his people, who have their eyes fixed on the unknown future. As Karl

Rahner wrote: 'No planning of the Church's future in the next decade can relieve us of the necessity of going forward into a future that cannot be planned, of risk, of danger, and of hope in the incalculable grace of God.'[4]

2

BIBLE

THE WORD OF GOD?

IN ATHENS in the heyday of classical Greece, boys received their schooling on the basis of a core curriculum. This included reading, writing, music, physical education and, as the foundation for all study, the works of Homer and other ancient poets. They had to memorise long passages from the Odyssey and the Iliad because these stories of gods and heroes provided basic clues to the meaning of life and the values by which good citizens should conduct themselves.

Similarly every great religion provides for its adherents a core curriculum as a foundation study. If you enter a mosque you will probably hear an imam or devout layman reciting long passages from the Koran, probably spoken from memory. The Salman Rushdie affair was a stern reminder of the powerful role the Islamic Word of God takes in the religious and political life of the Muslim people. For the Hebrew people the sacred Scriptures known as the Law (Torah), the Prophets and the Writings provided the authentic Word of God upon which their national and personal lives must be founded. In the Christian Church there is a similar authority accorded to the Old and New Testaments, written words which occupy a unique place and from which can be derived an understanding of God and his purpose for the world he has created. Article 6 of the Church of England asserts that the Holy Scriptures contain 'all things necessary to salvation: so that whatsoever is not read therein is not to be required of any man, that it should be believed as an article of the faith'. In the Westminster Abbey service of Coronation, in the time-honoured Anglican ritual, the newly crowned monarch is presented with a copy of the Bible with the words: 'We present to you this Book, the most valuable thing this world affords. Here is wisdom: this is the royal Law; these are the lively oracles of God.' Does the book really merit such extravagant claims? Can it really command such obedience?

In most churches today the reading from the Bible, however obscure and primitive the chosen passage may seem to be, is followed by the statement, 'This is the Word of God.' There are occasions when it is very tempting to reply, 'Is it?'. What precisely is this volume which can be so extravagantly described as God's mouthpiece? It is a collection of sixty-six books of varying lengths, dates, styles, authorship and subject matter. The books vary in quality from one to another. They include theology, prophecy, liturgy, moral and social instruction and personal reminiscences. Much of what we now have in written form had its origins in an oral tradition handed down from generation to generation in various Middle East countries over many centuries. Many of the names which appear as authors did not write the books attributed to them. Moses did not write the first five books of the Old Testament. Isaiah wrote only one third of the prophecy which bears his name. Solomon did not write the Song of Songs. David wrote only a few (if any) of the psalms. Paul did not write all the epistles purported to come from his pen. The apostle John did not write the book of Revelation and it is doubted whether he wrote the fourth Gospel. Many books are of composite material from different centuries and often clumsily stitched together to produce manifest contradictions, as in the two creation stories in Genesis. There are many improbabilities, such as Methuselah living to be 969 years old, the sun staying still to enable Joshua to complete a battle before evening, Balaam's talking donkey, Elijah's chariot of fire and Jonah in the belly of a great fish. The New Testament includes equal improbabilities. Was Jesus really conceived without semen from a human father? Did he really feed five thousand people to their satisfaction with a few loaves of bread and a small helping of fish? Did he really walk on water? Was his tomb really empty after his death by crucifixion?

It is not only the content of the Bible which raises huge questions. The Old Testament books were written in Hebrew, the New Testament in Greek. None of the writers thought of themselves as contributing to the making of a Holy Book. Only as the years went by were all these bits and pieces from so many sources, written for so many different occasions, collected together, edited, selected, finally to form the canonical books of the Old and New Testaments. None of the original manuscripts remain. All we have are copies made from copies, many times over, with all the errors of transmission, obscurities and mistranslations inevitable in any documents which have survived from ancient times. The miracle is that so much material, and in such good shape, remains at our disposal so many centuries after these writings first saw the light of day.

Yet the awkward question remains. Can we really call this hotch-potch of material the Word of God? If the Bible is really supposed to be the supreme way in which God reveals himself to mankind, why did he choose such a hit-and-miss way of doing it? Could not the God who made the universe with such order and complexity have thought of a better way of revealing himself than this? Why did he trust himself to the uncertain vagaries of human memory, authorship and language? Why did he trust himself to editors, translators, publishers, scribes and printers? Why did he take the likely risk of manuscripts being mislaid, miscopied, misunderstood, so that we cannot be quite certain when we read the Bible how close we are to the original author's meaning? If we go to a number of expert Bible commentaries to discover the significance of a specific chapter or verse, we may not get exactly the same information from all of them. Bishop David Jenkins and Dr Billy Graham may derive quite different interpretations from an identical passage. Are there great sections of Scripture which have not survived but would have had pride of place in our Bible if they had done so? There are two surviving letters from St Paul to the Corinthians in the New Testament, but it is generally believed by scholars that there were two others which have not been preserved for us. Did he write other letters which were destroyed by Roman soldiers in an anti-Christian pogrom? We do not know. Questions such as these remind us of the slender thread upon which the risk-taking God has chosen to reveal himself to us in a book described as 'the most valuable thing this world affords'. The very concept of a complex work of ancient literature handed down over many centuries to be a primary source of divine revelation, reveals to us a God prepared to take enormous risks. As we shall discover later, the content of the Bible, the investigations of science, the history of the Church and the examination of our situation now, all point to the same conclusion.

To many Christians with a strongly held faith the concept of a risk-taking God seems to be offensive. If God intended the revelation of himself through his Word to be unhindered by human error, misadventure or natural disaster, surely nothing could thwart his purpose. Faith in the overriding providence of God compels such people to hold to a strong belief in the inerrancy of Scripture and the infallability of its message. If the Bible is truly the Word of God, written by his hand, dictated to the authors by the Holy Spirit, even down to the last syllable and punctuation mark, it follows that there can be no possibility of error, no passage which does not contain profound truths for our edification, and nothing which cannot be eventually understood in faith. Even those passages which appear obscure or contradictory, can be accepted as part of God's plan, to be received in faith until all is made clear in his own good time. God does not take risks with his faithful people. This view of the Bible attracts many people. There can be no denying the power which springs from some of those who hold this absolutist conviction.

Those who take a different view of biblical inspiration, who wish to study Scripture in the light of textual criticism and in the perspective of historical discipline and scientific investigation, are tempted to take a superior view of the fundamentalists, thinking them to be naive and ignorant. It cannot be denied that there is some truth in the judgement. Yet there is also truth in the fact that those who take the words of the Bible literally as inspired in every detail, often display a knowledge of the Bible and a deep affection for it which can shame those who consider themselves to be more enlightened. Critical scholarship is essential for an understanding of what kind of work the Bible actually is, and offers a deeper interpretation of its message than is available for those who deliberately reject the help that scholarship can bring. Yet the God who takes risks appears to allow his Good News to be understood and proclaimed in many different ways. The whole Church is the richer in experience for having both academic Bible scholars searching for the truth and fundamentalists loving the message and the words that convey it to them. If seekers after the truth of the ways that God has chosen to reveal himself could combine the honesty and critical skills of the scholar with the enthusiasm and commitment of the Bible 'literalist', the Church might be enriched by a great outpouring of new spiritual power and understanding. By either route God is found to be an explorer in action within the ups and downs of the human situation, subjecting himself to risk-taking in the world that he has created. Those who wish to respond to the divine initiative must be risk-takers and explorers themselves.

If God seems to have taken considerable risks in the trans-mission of the written records which were to become our Holy Bible, the actual way in which that revelation was given appears to have been equally precarious. It seems odd that God's chosen method of making himself known should have been liable to so much misunderstanding and so many different interpretations. But how else could he have done it? Human beings cannot visualise concepts which lie beyond the experience of the time and space in which they live. When people talk about God they have only the language of human speech with which to do it. When they want to describe God they must use the imagery of everyday existence. So they have learned to speak of God as father (or mother), judge, king, lord, shepherd, friend. Hosea used the parent-child relationship as a way of describing God's care for his people. Isaiah told his hearers to think of God as their husband. The Bible is full of such human analogies as a convenient way of describing man's experience of God. Yet this way of talking about God, although the only way we have, is full of risks. In human experience some fathers are inadequate, some judges are harsh, some kings are powerless, some friends let you down. Sunday school books show sentimental pictures of the Good Shepherd. A visit to the nearest sheep market may give a rather different impression of what shepherding is really like. It is often pointed out that children who are abused by their parents are unlikely to gain a very attractive picture of God as 'our Father'. To children who have been cruelly treated at home, such a picture of God is either meaningless or even repulsive. Some people want to argue that to attempt to describe God in language derived from human relationships is so fraught with risk that it is better to avoid it altogether. Better to talk about him in more abstract terms:

> Immortal, invisible, God only wise,
> In light inaccessible hid from our eyes.

Yet most people need to visualise God more concretely and in personal terms. The Bible takes the risk of encouraging them to do so. It was a risk that Jesus himself took when he taught his disciples to pray to God as father, and used the intimate childish word *Abba*. The precariousness of the relationship between language and experience is one of the inevitable risks which God had to take if his relevation of himself to mankind was to be transmitted, with any meaning at all, through the use of language, the currency of human intercourse.

It is the evidence of the Bible, both in the Old Testament and in the New, that God has revealed his nature in a way firmly implanted within the contemporary context of the actual lives of individuals and communities who became aware of his impact upon them. The historical nature of divine revelation carries many risks, not only because the meaning of words frequently changes, but the presuppositions which underlie language become obsolete and unintelligible to future generations. So the word of God comes to us in the Bible through the myths, prayers, poems, science, theology and (above all) through the personal experiences of peoples who lived in parts of the Middle East over a period of two thousand years. What they had to tell us about their vision of God is enshrined in a body of literature which has survived to make a lasting contribution to the human quest for religious truth. But every page grows out of the discoveries made by individuals and groups firmly rooted in their own time and under the influence of their own culture. Every page of Scripture is rooted in its own contemporary situation. If the greatest benefit is to be had from these astonishing pages in a way that makes sense to us in our own time, we need to cultivate the ability, as far as we are able, to put ourselves into the shoes of those who first penned these sentences. This is the purpose of all serious Bible study, from the most advanced academic work in a university theology department to the producers of easy daily Bible reading notes or the preacher deciding what to talk about in his cathedral or village church next Sunday. God's plan to reveal himself in a continuous historical process is the risk he has taken, and which he continues to take. Anyone who wants to come to a clearer understanding of God must be willing to join in this on-going process of exploration.

The explorer meets problems in the very opening pages of the Old Testament, with strange tales about creation in six days, Adam and Eve and a talking snake, a universal flood, and much else. Scholars whose job it is to study these things, and churchgoers accustomed to hearing them read aloud on Sundays, may forget what a hindrance these old tales may prove to be for the honest enquirer after faith. To start reading the Bible from the beginning (which is not the right place to start) is to find yourself being plunged immediately into a world of fantasy. It would seem that God has chosen a very risky way of making himself known if we are to take seriously the claim that this is his Word.

Recently I met a student who had taken his first degree in some branch of physics and was now in a university in the south of England working for his doctorate. He was obviously an intelligent young man. Our conversation turned to religion. Was he a churchgoer? Did he call himself a Christian? In each case the answer was in the negative. He said he found it difficult to believe. When I asked him to explain further, he said that it seemed to him to be impossible to accept the story of creation and Adam and Eve. So an intelligent young scientist, genuinely anxious to find a faith to live by, is turned off his quest by the opening chapters of the Bible. There must be thousands like him. No one had told him that these stories have their origins in ancient Middle East civilisations, much older than the Hebrews. No one had explained to him that they are remnants from an age when religious and moral truths were expressed in the form of myths, legends and bizarre stories. Here in the early stories of Genesis is a fascinating and enthralling reminder of how primitive people tried to find answers to the questions posed by everyday existence. How did the world come into being? Why are there so many plants, trees and animals and how did they get their names? What were the first human beings like? Why are people ashamed of nakedness? How did the first murder happen? Why do people speak so many different languages and find it so hard to understand one another? Ancient peoples wove wonderful stories in their attempts to find satisfactory answers to these questions.

Some of these tales became part of the folk lore of the Hebrew people whose ancestors lived in the lands which we now call Iran and Iraq, from which many of these myths and legends had their origin. The people of the Bible handed down these tales from generation to generation, adding fresh insights as their understanding of God developed through the rough-and-tumble years of their adventurous history. Each great event in their national story inspired them to develop these old inherited traditions, making additions and refinements in tune with their new theological understanding. Eventually they came to piece together these various traditions from the past to make a single continuous narrative as best they could. By modern literary standards their editing of the material might seem rather careless. It is not difficult to find a number of contradictions and repetitions, such as two different accounts of creation in the first two chapters of Genesis. Yet these stories remain a joy to read and a source of inspiration. But they prove a risky introduction to faith. In what sense can they be called the Word of God?

The genius of these early chapters of Genesis is that they take hold of this primitive material and weave a narrative which is not a scientific text book about the origin of things but a theological affirmation of God's purpose in creation. So these passages are carefully studied today, and read aloud in public worship, because they are an invaluable witness to the growing awareness of God and the response to him of successive generations of men and women who belonged to a nation with a genius for religion. As will be discussed in the next chapter, we do not look in these writings for answers to scientific questions which are the appropriate study for scientists. The Bible writers had no access to the scientific information available to us. The Bible has a different story to tell. To discover what it has to say to us living at the end of the twentieth century, we have to learn to approach it not simply as a 'book full of stories', or an anthology of fascinating ancient Middle East literature, nor even as a history of its times – though it is all these things. Nor must we be so dazzled by such phrases as 'the inspired Word of God' that we treat it as a kind of book of magic. We have to approach it as a book which invites us to take it seriously as an invitation to explore into God, bringing with us all those faculties we can summon up of intelligence, wonder, honest questioning, imagination, conscience and expectation. We have to marvel at the fact that God has taken the mighty risk of entrusting to us as an instrument of revelation about himself, this extraordinary, inspiring, puzzling, sometimes obscure, sometimes shocking hotch-potch of writings that some people dare to call his Word. Only as we learn to explore it in this spirit can we begin to discover how the living God can speak to us through the words of people long since dead.

As we read the early chapters of Genesis we must put scientific questions on one side. This will clear our minds to find magnificent food for thought as we explore what they have to tell us about the relationship between chaos and order in the world, about the responsibility of human beings for the world of nature with which they share this planet, about the mystery of sexual intercourse between men and women and how that relationship can be broken by disobedience to the divine will. We can read in the story of Cain and Abel about breakdown in the workplace when rivalry and jealousy fracture the harmony of co-operative enterprise. And the myth of the tower of Babel is discovered to be a remarkably penetrating parable of the dangers of national pride and ambition. It is a tale of power-hungry politicians, ambitious to build a city and a tower reaching to heaven (and thus usurping God's authority), with their desire to make a name for themselves. As we read it we quickly recognise the relevance of this story to our contemporary international, national and municipal scene. The end result of their presumption is that they no longer understand one another. They talk at cross purposes, they 'no longer speak the same language'.

Careful reading of Old Testament myths and legends leads students to different interpretations of their significance for our own times. This is a necessary part of the divine risk. It is his way of making his 'word' available to each new situation in each new generation. This is the open-ended way in which we must approach the Bible. There is no 'correct' interpretation of the puzzles which the Bible sets us. It is not like a book of mathematical problems with the right answers printed in the back. God's word in Scripture is given in such a way that it can be the vehicle of revelation available throughout the unfolding process of personal and community history. But it is a risky way.

PRECARIOUS HISTORY

The Old Testament is the record of the unfolding of the history of the Hebrew people and their growing awareness of God and of the way he acts in the everyday lives of individuals and nations. It is a puzzling and often confusing story. William Cowper wrote how God 'moves in a mysterious way his wonders to perform', and expressed a belief that 'God is his own interpreter and he will make it plain.' Yet the Bible record is often very far from plain, and often, far from being his own interpreter, God invites us to explore the material for ourselves and make the best sense of it we can. Even the best Bible scholars know that so long as we are here on earth, the search for meaning will continue. Exploring the unknown and taking risks with our faith must be an essential element in the religious pilgrimage. The Bible provides us with a wealth of material for that adventure.

It was with remarkable insight that the Bible writers dared to re-tell the old story of the universal flood as a way of describing God's sense of failure at what seemed to him to be the lack of success in his experiment of creation.

> Yahweh saw that the wickedness of man was great on the earth, and that the thoughts in his heart fashioned nothing but wickedness all day long. Yahweh regretted having made man on the earth, and his heart grieved. 'I will rid the earth's face of man, my own creation,' Yahweh said 'and of the animals also, reptiles too, and the birds of heaven; for I regret having made them.'[1]

Like an artist painting a picture which does not work out as he had planned, so that he is tempted to destroy it and start afresh, so the Bible writers dared to picture their God. Although God has a plan for mankind and knows that risks are involved, yet he is prepared to go back to the beginning and start again when the experiment looks like being a failure. In righteous Noah and his family God sees a faint glimmer of hope to keep his experiment going. The fairy-tale fable of Noah's ark, a subject suitable for a children's toy, contains within it a profound theological insight into the character of God. He not only risks his experiment of creation going wrong. He also risks giving it a second chance, as if only a number of failed experiments can lead to eventual success. In the next chapter we shall see how scientific research corroborates this picture of trial and error in the divine purpose.

The Bible story continues with down-to-earth realism. Noah and his family, with the remnant of creation which survived the flood, emerge from the ark to begin life again in the brave new world. But once again the divine experiment takes a turn for the worse. Noah is discovered by his shocked family lying stark naked on the ground by his tent and in a drunken stupor.[2] The Bible writers were never ones to cover up the less attractive side of the human experiment. And they did not hesitate to blame God for taking the risk of allowing the seamy side of life to happen. Sometimes they thought that God had taken too many risks and that life would be much better if he had kept a firmer control over the things that happen.

The accounts we are given of such leading Old Testament characters as Abraham and Moses show that they had to take great risks for God because God took great risks with them. Whether Abraham was an actual individual or the personification of a tribe is an open question. He represents the beginning of the biblical history through which God was to reveal himself uniquely to his chosen people. The story begins with a journey into the unknown: 'He set out not knowing where he was going.' He is presented throughout the Bible as a prototype figure who knew that faith involves a journey into risk. The curious story of the occasion when he nearly sacrificed his son Isaac because he thought that was what God wanted, indicates an inner conflict which Abraham had to face when he arrived in Canaan where the heathen worshippers sacrificed children to placate their various deities. Abraham must have wondered whether this meant that the pagans were more fervent in the worship of their gods than he was with the animal sacrifices which he was wont to offer to his God Yahweh. There were other conflicts to be faced to do with finding appropriate living space for his rapidly expanding tribe. There were domestic problems of marriage and family life. The Abraham story sets the scene for much that follows in the Bible. It was when people took the risk of pulling up their roots and moving into fresh situations that they gained new insights into the character and activity of their risk-taking God. So we read of Moses on his way to the promised land; Ezekiel among the exiles in Babylon; Jesus leading his disciples from the comparative safety of Galilee to face the dangers of the city of Jerusalem; Peter travelling from Joppa to Caesarea to discover the Spirit of God alive and active in the household of a Roman army officer; Paul making his momentous journey to Damascus from which he set out on his mission to Europe. Each journey was full of risk. Each journey took the religious quest a significant step forward. The significance of this discovery through moving forward into new situations will be discussed in later chapters.

Popular evangelists often seek to sell their wares as a soft option. Once you accept Jesus into your life, they say, you will be given a blessed assurance in which your doubts and anxieties will be removed and everything in your garden will be lovely. This is not the witness of Scripture. Moses accepted God's call to lead the people into the promised land and that was the beginning of his troubles. Not only did he face periodic bouts of rebellion from the 'chosen people', but on more than one occasion he lost not only faith in himself but also in God. David the anointed one, selected to be the great charismatic leader of his people, succumbed to gross moral failure, faced civil war initiated from within his own family, and died a disappointed old man. Solomon, promised by God to be given the divine gift of wisdom, was so unwise in his political judgements and in his matrimonial affairs, that on his death his kingdom was fatally split in two. In painting a picture of those who had heard the call of God and promised to obey it, the Bible is scrupulously honest. There is no facile optimism or promise of easy success. Nowhere is this more evident than in the Psalms which, as Gordon Mursell has pointed out in a valuable study,[3] contain many prayers of vigorous protest against God. 'Why do you stand aside? Why hide from us now the times are hard?', one of them questions. Another dares to accuse God of breaking his covenant with his people. Another suggests that God has gone to sleep: 'Wake up, Lord, why are you asleep? Awake, do not abandon us for ever.' Another has the courage or impudence to enquire whether God is losing his memory or suffering from some kind of paralysis:

> Has God forgotten to be gracious,
> has he in anger withheld his mercies?
> 'Has his right hand', I said, 'lost its grasp?
> Does it hang powerless, the arm of the Most High?'
>   (NEB)

Gordon Mursell comments: 'Their relationship with God was a two-way process involving not just reverence, not just passivity, but protest whatever the cost and risk involved.'

The story of the chosen people of God in the Old Testament moves from one crisis to another. There are few moments of peace and prosperity. Even when at first things seem to be going well, as in the prosperous days of Solomon, trouble is being stored up for the future. The risk-taking God does not protect his special people either from their own folly or from the ups and downs of political, economic and social rough and tumble. It is not surprising that they were often indignant about the way they thought God was treating them. If he took risks with them, they had no hesitation in taking the risk of shouting back at him. It was, in particular, the great series of prophets who came to understand the remarkable truth that it was in the risky periods of their personal and national lives that the voice of God, speaking to them in judgement and in mercy, was most clearly heard. The experience of a disastrous break-up in his marriage and his readiness to go to any lengths to win his wife back to their home again, made Hosea realise the depths of God's love for his faithless people. It was the tragic death following leprosy of Uzziah, the successful king of Judah, that inspired his friend and adviser Isaiah to hear a fresh vision of God's purpose for a bereaved nation. The catastrophic fall of Jerusalem and the enforced exile of all the most influential people to become the hostages of their captors in Babylon, led Ezekiel and the unknown prophet whose words appear in Isaiah 40–55 to explore with new understanding the concept of the universality of God's rule, and to see suffering as part of his redemptive purpose for his people. The same God who in the Old Testament used the risks of history to enable people to learn more about him and themselves, is revealed in greater fulness in the life and death of Jesus of Nazareth.

RISKY INTERVENTION

The author of the letter to the Hebrews links the New Testament with the Old in a brilliant opening sentence designed to catch the attention of the reader: 'In various times in the past and in various different ways, God spoke to our ancestors through the prophets; but in our own time, the last days, he has spoken to us through his Son.' We have been arguing that the Old Testament presents the picture of a God who takes risks with his people and expects them to take risks with him in their search for faith. We shall not be surprised to find a similar emphasis in the life and teaching of Jesus Christ, reflected also in the experience of the first Christians as they struggled to bring the Church into existence. The whole corpus of New Testament writings spans less than a century. Its earliest material consists of letters written by St Paul and others, addressed to small Christian communities living in the major cities in the Graeco-Roman world of the first century. These letters are living documents of the greatest historical and theological importance, as they give us a vivid picture of men and women trying to work out the significance for their lives of a faith derived from a Jewish teacher who lived and died in Palestine and whom very few of them had ever seen. They were claiming that what this man taught, and the facts of his life, were giving them an entirely new understanding of God and of themselves. We get a wonderful insight into their attempts to come to terms with this remarkable new faith, as they searched for the appropriate language with which to put it into words. Paul must have expressed the emotions of many of those early pioneers of the faith when he wrote, 'All I can say is that I forget the past and I strain ahead for what is still to come'.[4] This was true to the adventurous spirit of the founding fathers,

Abraham and Moses, always pressing forward towards the unknown future.

The Epistles are concerned with the impact of Jesus of Nazareth on the life of these first Christian communities. It is strange how little they tell us about Jesus himself. Apart from his crucifixion and resurrection the historical facts of his life are totally ignored. It seems as if the impact of Jesus was of greater importance to them than information about his life and teaching. This gives rise to some fascinating questions. For our knowledge of the earthly life of Jesus we have to rely on the four Gospels. These had not yet been written by the time Paul wrote the last of his letters. If the Gospels had not survived, and we had to rely on the Epistles, we would be almost entirely ignorant of all the familiar facts of the Jesus story. There is something very precarious about the fact that the story has come down to us at all. Today, biographies are amongst the most popular forms of literature. They appear in the bookshops even while their subjects are still alive. Works of this kind were unknown in New Testament times. The fact that many Christians expected Jesus to come back to earth in their own time would, in any event, make the writing of an official biography unnecessary. It was only as the original eyewitnesses were beginning to die that it began to seem sensible to collect together some first-hand memories recalling major events in the life story of Jesus, and reminiscences of his teaching. So slowly, over a number of years, gospels began to take shape with the purpose, in St Luke's words, of drawing up 'accounts of the events that have taken place among us, exactly as these were handed down to us by those who from the outset were eyewitnesses and ministers of the word'.[5]

Four of these accounts survive, compiled by different people at different times. Some passages in the first three Gospels are more or less identical, evidence that they used a common source or copied from one another. The fourth Gospel is written in a style all of its own. Some of the most important events in the life of Jesus appear only in one or two of the Gospels and are unaccountably ignored by the others. Only Matthew and Luke have accounts of the conception and birth of Jesus, and their accounts differ. Only Luke includes the parables of the Good Samaritan and the Prodigal Son. Only John tells of the most dramatic of the miracles, the raising of Lazarus from the dead. There are slight differences in the list of names of the twelve apostles in the various Gospels. All four Gospels devote considerable space to the story of the passion of Christ and his resurrection, but their accounts vary and do not tally easily together. Only Luke and Matthew mention the ascension.

These variations and discrepancies lead New Testament scholars to question how accurate our knowledge of the life of Jesus can be. It is improbable that those who say that the whole story of Jesus is simply a legend or a myth can be right. This strains credibility. But it is equally unlikely that it can be accepted with any certainty that every word in the Gospels is literal historical fact. In between these two extremes scholars of repute differ widely in their quest for the Jesus of history. The Gospels were written by men of faith and in good faith, but they were not historians as we now understand the writing of history. They were evangelists, making use of any stories, anecdotes, memories, sermons, prayers, reports which came to them from the past and which could now be used to bear witness to their faith. Biblical scholarship cannot invalidate the faith of those Gospel writers. It can help us to understand more easily the nature of the material they used.

There are many things about Jesus we do not know. We would like to know what Jesus looked like. We would like to know about his boyhood, adolescence and young manhood. What were his hobbies? Did he have girl friends? There must have been many more parables, miracles and other striking events which have not been recorded. The amount of detailed biographical information we have about him is tantalisingly small. The greater part of his life is completely hidden from us. It is tempting to complain that if God really wanted to reveal himself through the life and death of a man called Jesus, why did he not make certain that what actually happened was so well recorded and authenticated that it could be accepted without question or doubt by all people for all time? Albert Schweitzer said that the Jesus of history must be 'for our time a stranger and an enigma'. It is obvious that the Church would not have come into existence if some of those who knew Jesus in the flesh were not absolutely convinced that he was a man for their own time, and one greatly needed. On the basis of their conviction, and the records they have left us of his teachings, miracles, death and rising to life, we are called to discover the significance of all that for ourselves in our own time. If this leaves much room for doubt and exploration, it is the price we have to pay as followers of an historically revealed religion rather than an abstract philosophical one. This is the risk-taking method God has chosen to make himself known.

If we look at the Gospel accounts of the life of Jesus we find, as we might expect, a considerable element of risk-taking as the story proceeds. Whether or not the story of the virginal conception of Jesus is a fact of history, it appears in two of the Gospels and must have been accepted in some circles at an early date. Matthew's comment that, when Joseph discovered that Mary was pregnant, 'being a man of honour and wanting to spare her publicity, (he) decided to divorce her informally', suggests that God was prepared to take a calculated risk of scandal at the start of what was to be the peak point in the divine revelation.

The account of the temptation in the wilderness must have been given to his closest followers by Jesus himself.[6] It is an extraordinary description of the conflict within himself at the outset of his public ministry. Would he best succeed by helping to solve the economic problems of his impoverished nation? Would a political campaign be a better way, leading a nationalist revolt against the Roman occupying forces to drive them out of the country? Would a religious wonder-working campaign at the heart of the inner city achieve his purpose more speedily by appearing to fulfil widely acclaimed prophecies? These three risks were rejected in favour of an even greater risk, which was to lead him to death by crucifixion.

Another risk which faced Jesus was the choice of his closest disciples who were to collaborate with him in his ministry. About some of the twelve apostles we have little or no knowledge. We can only be certain of the names of nine of them. Because an assortment of names are scattered among the Gospels, one commentator has suggested that it requires 'the most ingenious juggling to reduce the number to twelve'. Jesus seems to have been prepared to take great risks in choosing some of the men whose names we do know. Judas Iscariot, the betrayer, is one example. Simon the Zealot and Matthew the tax collector must have caused some anxious moments in the company, the former being a member of the extreme anti-Roman nationalist party, the latter a man who earned his living by collaborating with the hated occupying power. Peter, whom Jesus rather surprisingly nicknames the Rock, denied his master three times with vehement oaths, and at the critical time joined all the others in running away. The subsequent history of the Church shows how God continued and still continues to take risks in trusting people who are not worthy of his trust.

Jesus was prepared to take risks both with his reputation and his safety. Matthew took great pleasure in introducing him to his disreputable friends and noting how much he relished being in their company. He seems to have enjoyed talking to officers in the Roman army who were regarded as unwelcome foreigners, and to Samaritans who were considered heretics by the orthodox. In his long conversation with a Samaritan woman he was breaking two taboos simultaneously.[7] Nor was Jesus averse to using strong language in passing judgement on the established Church and State. He described King Herod Agrippa as 'that fox',[8] and said that the leaders of the ecclesiastical world were like 'whitewashed tombs that look handsome on the outside, but inside are full of dead men's bones and every kind of corruption'.[9] Risky talk from the lips of a popular religious campaigner.

Jesus was also ready to take risks in his chosen method of teaching. He was the least dogmatic or moralistic of preachers. In consequence, much of what he taught was misunderstood. The heart of his message was to proclaim what life would be like if people took God's will seriously enough to be able to apply it to all the ordinary events and relationships of everyday life. Following Old Testament precedent, he called this the kingdom of God and taught his followers to pray daily for its coming on earth. Much of his teaching was given through the vehicle of stories drawn from secular life. He talked about weddings, wine bottling, highway robbery, unemployment, burglary, housekeeping, farming, family life, commerce, accounting. Some of the stories raised controversial issues (the Good Samaritan), some had surprise endings (the Prodigal Son), some were shocking (the Unjust Stewart), some revealed a wry humour such as the tale of the ten bridesmaids, the man knocking his friend up at midnight, the widow pestering a stubborn judge

before he finally gave judgement in her favour. It is generally
believed that Jesus left his stories unexplained. Telling people
to work things out for themselves ('ears to hear') is a far more
effective way of getting a message across than concluding with
dogmatic moralising propositions. It is a risky method of teaching. Two thousand years after they were first told, we are still
discussing what these stories mean for us in our own time. That
is their value.

Nowhere in the Gospels is the risk-taking God so clearly
revealed as in their closing chapters. We see Jesus deliberately
choosing to go from the comparative comfort and safety of
Galilee to the dangers of Jerusalem. He knew that he would
face hostility from the authorities and the possibility of betrayal
by his friends. He must have guessed that there was a reasonable
chance of being arrested by the Roman police and put on trial
before the Consul's high court. If he knew that he was the Son
of God and that he was to be crucified and rise again on the
third day, we have to say that the risk element would have been
minimal. There would always have been a happy ending in
sight. But if we are right in thinking that he was truly a human
being like the rest of us, and not God play-acting in human
disguise, then we are left with the staggering possibility of a
God whose plan for the salvation of his creation involved for
himself appalling risk. If Jesus on his knees in Gethsemane,
sweating out his prayer to the Father to 'take this cup from me',
already knew the Easter outcome, would this not have been an
empty charade? If the words mean what they say, we are taken
breathtakingly into the mystery of the risk-taking God. Later,
the cry from the cross, 'My God, my God, why have you
deserted me?', shows that the risk-taking continued to the very
end. In his last moments of consciousness, Jesus is still daring
to express the purpose of God for humanity. There is no happy
ending until risk has been explored to the ultimate degree.

3

CREATION

THE SEARCH FOR MEANING

WHEN PEOPLE FIRST began asking questions about the origins of the world and the meaning of life, they found the answers they needed in the old tales of gods and heroes which formed the foundation heritage of every ancient civilisation. The stories which circulated three thousand years before Christ in countries of the Middle East told how at the beginning of time order emerged out of chaos, how the natural world came into being, how man and woman came to occupy a special place in creation. These stories eventually found their way into the book of Genesis, refined (as we have already seen) by the religious experience of centuries. But the stories remained myths, full of profound and poetic symbolism, but with no pretence to being scientific explanations. The scientific approach to knowledge, which we take for granted, had not yet arrived.

Further west, in the countries surrounding the Aegean Sea, the civilisation of the Greeks had developed its own myths of gods and heroes to explain the origin of things and the bewildering contradictions in human character and experience. At about the same time that the Hebrew prophets were at work, Homer was writing the Iliad and the Odyssey, which became the foundation subjects for Greek religious education. Not only do they tell marvellous stories but (like the biblical myths) they explore the fundamental concerns of life and death, good and evil. But soon Greek thinkers were no longer content with the old stories, and in the seventh century BC, in cities along the coast of Asia Minor (where six hundred years later St Paul was founding a number of churches) we find a remarkable series of mathematicians, astronomers, physicists and philosophers who were beginning to explore more profoundly the origins of creation and the meaning of life. They asked questions about the nature of the physical world around them. What is the stuff of material existence? How did it come into being? What is it that holds everything together? They dared to question the validity of the old myths and began to develop the scientific method of exploration, experiment and rational thought. They were ready to pursue new paths, taking courage to turn their backs on the old myths even though they would continue to have a place in the national culture. They were prepared to follow false trails, turning back when necessary. What they were seeking for was some kind of hypothesis which would make sense of the vast variety of phenomena with which they were confronted in themselves and in the natural world around them. Is there some ultimate substance or power which gives order and unity to the whole universe? In answer to their questions they began to use words like Spirit or Breath (*pneuma*) and Word (*logos*) as ways of describing the divine principle which they were certain gave unity and meaning to the whole universe. Both these words were to appear in the New Testament five centuries later, to describe the activity of God.

The brilliant pioneering work of these philosophical scientists was to find an echo in a remarkable passage in the book of Wisdom in the Old Testament Apocrypha. Written in Alexandria in the century before the birth of Christ, it reflects the marriage of Greek with Hebrew thought. In one section of the book which repays careful study in a good modern translation, the author prays that God will enable him to speak as he would wish and express thoughts worthy of his gifts.

We are indeed in his hand, we ourselves and our words,
with all our understanding, too, and technical knowledge.
It was he who gave me true knowledge of all that is,
who taught me the structure of the world and the
    properties of the elements,
the beginning, end and middle of the times,
the alternation of the solstices and the succession of
    the seasons,

the revolution of the year and the position of the stars,
the natures of animals and the instincts of wild beasts,
the powers of spirits and the mental processes of men,
the varieties of plants and the medical properties of roots.
All that is hidden, and all that is plain, I have come
    to know,
instructed by Wisdom who designed them all.[1]

So this author sees the work of God revealed in philosophy, physics, medicine, chemistry, astronomy, history, zoology, meteorology, botany, pharmacology.

Sir Christopher Wren died in 1723 and over the north door of his masterpiece, St Paul's Cathedral in London, the famous epitaph in his memory is inscribed: *si monumentum requiris, circumspice* (if you would see his monument, look about you). This is how the scientists and philosophers of the seventeenth-century period of the Enlightenment in England saw the works of nature which were becoming increasingly revealed by rapid developments in scientific research. If you want to see evidence of God, look at the world about you. Joseph Addison, who died four years before Wren, voiced the optimistic faith of those who half a century earlier had founded the Royal Society for the Improvement of Natural Knowledge. In a poem which still appears in some hymn books, he sings of the orderly movements of the heavenly bodies as bearing witness to the power and rationality of the Creator God:

> The spacious firmament on high,
> With all the blue ethereal sky,
> And spangled heavens, a shining frame
> Their great Original proclaim.
> The unwearied sun from day to day
> Does his Creator's power display,
> And publishes to every land
> The works of an almighty hand.

A second stanza rhapsodises on the night sky, the movement of the moon, planets and stars, concluding with a sentiment which the early philosophers of Greece might have been happy to share with the religious rationalists of eighteenth-century England:

> In reason's ear they all rejoice,
> And utter forth a glorious voice,
> Forever singing as they shine
> 'The hand that made us is divine'.

The founder members of the Royal Society were a remarkable group of men who sought to match their discoveries in the scientific field with their conviction as devout Christian believers. Robert Boyle, whose hydrostatic laws still puzzle schoolchildren in their physics laboratories, wrote books about theology as well as about science. Much of his writing was an attempt to vindicate a harmony between the Christian faith and scientific research. John Ray, a field naturalist who wrote important descriptions of plants and animals, also produced a work on the 'theology of insects' in which he attempted to demonstrate the intricate wonder of the Creator's design by examining in detail the physiology and habits of the insect kingdom. He wrote that there was no occupation more worthy and delightful than to contemplate the beauteous works of nature and so to honour the infinite wisdom and goodness of God. Sir Isaac Newton, the greatest of all English scientists, held a similar view. He claimed that the scientist who studied how the universe was ordered and controlled was 'thinking God's thoughts after him'. He wrote that 'the most beautiful system of the sun, planets and comets could only proceed from the counsel and dominion of an intelligent powerful Being. God endures for ever and is everywhere present, and by existing always and everywhere, he constitutes duration and space.'

Until the middle of the nineteenth century this argument from design was thought to be all that science could say in support of traditional Christian orthodoxy in its theology of creation. The year 4004 BC was accepted as the precise date for the creation of the world, and was inserted into many editions of the Authorised Version of the Bible. The orderly pattern of the six days of creation was generally thought to be a true enough picture of the way God had worked. Towards the end of the eighteenth century William Paley, archdeacon of Taunton, summed up this conventional teaching in his immensely popular books, *Evidences of Christianity* (1794) and *Natural Theology* (1802), in which he examined the design apparent in the observable phenomena of nature, and drew from it his well-known analogy of the universe as a watch which had been put together and set in motion by the master watchmaker, the Creator of heaven and earth. This seemed to most people to be a safe and sound hypothesis. Chance was eliminated. Such a precise mechanistic view left no room for a God who, as we suggested in the previous chapter, appeared not only to take risks with his creation, but even to make mistakes.

In the century following Paley, scientific and theological questioning began to disturb this tranquil and satisfactory picture of a clockwork universe. In the middle years of the nineteenth century the Revd Baden Powell, father of the founder of the Boy Scout movement, was professor of geometry in the university of Oxford. In his book, *Revelation and Science*, he argued that recent geological discoveries were making it impossible to accept the Genesis account of creation as literal truth. He insisted vigorously in public (as very few clergyman at that time dared to do) that the Church had no right to claim infallibility in matters where science offered more convincing evidence. Already geologists were examining fossils which must have taken millions of years to form. The conventional wisdom that the earth was created in 4004 BC was flatly refuted by such discoveries. Some devout Christians, disturbed by this challenge to their faith in the inerrancy of Scripture, solved their dilemma by saying that it was obvious that God had put the fossils in the rocks in order to mislead the experts! There followed a long struggle on the part of the scientists to convince the public of the validity of their findings. Conservative churchmen fought a long and hard rearguard action against ideas that they were convinced were blasphemous. The more far-seeing of the theologians had an equally uphill task to persuade their more traditional colleagues that God does not only reveal himself through the pages of the Bible or through channels usually regarded as 'religious'; God has given the scientists the task of revealing him through their study of the world that he has created and in doing so has helped us all to broaden our understanding of the Creator himself. The argument continued throughout the second half of the nineteenth century as new discoveries came to light in biology and physics. It continued into the twentieth century and has not yet come to a full stop.

The dominating figure in the debate was Charles Darwin. A field naturalist, indefatigable traveller, keen observer, with a meticulous and logical mind, the more he studied the animal kingdom the more convinced he became that neither Genesis nor Archdeacon Paley had got it right. His conclusions reached the public in 1859 with his epoch-making *On the Origin of Species by Means of Natural Selection*, followed twelve years later by *The Descent of Man*. His theory of evolution and natural selection created a storm of discussion, with much vigorous disapproval from ecclesiastical quarters. Its basic tenets seem to most people today to be obvious. Darwin affirmed that all organisms have descended from one or several living species which in the long-distant past arose spontaneously. Species are derived from one another by a process of natural selection, with the best offspring surviving and, in their turn, procreating. Through this struggle for the survival of the fittest every living creature has evolved from lower to higher forms. Human beings owe their origin and development to the same biological processes. They are made of the same stuff and have evolved in the same way as the rest of creation.

It was this last proposition which sent shock waves to disturb the widely held belief in the inerrancy of the Bible and the literal truth of its creation stories. 'The principle of natural selection', said Samuel Wilberforce, Bishop of Oxford, 'is absolutely incompatible with the word of God.' Unlike Addison, Darwin did not see the necessity of postulating a Designer. Evolution occurred spontaneously through natural competition. There was no need for the intervention of a creator as each new species evolved.[2]

Darwinism came as a strong challenge to the views of the much-acclaimed Archdeacon Paley. The mechanistic watchmaker concept of Almighty God was giving way to the much less comfortable vision of the struggle for existence in nature, bringing with it an element of risk and chance in which the Creator himself is involved. Did this put in jeopardy the reassuring faith in divine providence, if God himself was now to be seen as somehow subject to chance? This raised awkward questions, which some good people found distasteful and therefore to be resisted as strongly as possible. Yet there were many churchmen ready to welcome the new horizons which were being opened up. The distinguished Cambridge New Testament scholar F. J. Hort wrote to his equally scholarly friend Bishop Westcott of Durham to enquire, 'Have you read Darwin? How I should like to talk to you about it. In spite of difficulties I am inclined to think of it as unanswerable. It is a treat to read such a book.' And J. R. Illingworth, country rector and prolific author of theological works, described the theory of evolution as 'an advance in our theological thinking, a definite increase in insight, a fresher and fuller appreciation of the many ways in which God fulfils himself.' It was men of this calibre who, in the face of new scientific knowledge which many of the devout found disturbing, were not afraid to take risks as they explored positively the impact of this new learning on traditional theological truth.

Today evolution as a basic concept of the way that nature works is widely accepted, though there continue to be disagreements on such particulars as the speed of evolution and the exact way in which it works. But science does not stay still. Modern developments in biology and physics have added new concepts, some of which are proving to be very revolutionary. Increasingly Christian thinkers have come to see that the concepts of evolutionary processes not only illuminate our understanding of how God works in creation, but also his purpose for the human race, revealed in the life and teaching of Jesus Christ, and ultimately to be fulfilled in the coming of his kingdom. Charles Raven was both an eminent theologian and a keen naturalist. He welcomed these developing theories of evolution and saw them reflected in his favourite passage from St Paul:

> From the beginning till now the entire creation, as we know, has been groaning in one great act of giving birth; and not only creation, but all of us who possess the first fruits of the Spirit, we too groan inwardly as we wait for our bodies to be set free.[3]

In an address on 'Christ and the World of Science' given in 1955 to students in McGill University, Canada, Canon Raven elaborated on this text. It tells us, he said, that creation is incomplete. It is like a great childbirth. God himself is involved in it: he is not like a spectator looking in from outside the world. If God is involved we need not be afraid. 'This concept is reconcilable all the way with an evolutionary concept of creation; not as an act but as a process; not as something complete, but as something in the making. It is a picture we can take to our scientific friends and dare to command their attention.'[4]

Raven published these lectures in the same year as the Jesuit priest Teilhard de Chardin died. Teilhard was a palaeontologist whose interest in evolution derived from a lifetime of study in fossils. Because his findings were in contradiction with the official views then held by the Roman Catholic Church, his masterpiece *The Phenomenon of Man* could not be published until after his death. It is a remarkable work, combining his scientific and theological knowledge, expressing his belief that it is appropriate to speak of the coming of Christ as the omega or ultimate point in the evolutionary process. He asks whether since the coming of Christ humankind may now become responsible enough to take control of the evolutionary process. 'Evolution has come to infuse new blood, so to speak, in the perspectives and aspirations of Christianity. In return, is not the Christian faith destined, is it now preparing, to save and even to take the place of evolution?'[5] Exploring these ideas brought Teilhard to conclusions which were fraught with risk. It is not surprising that his Church feared their publication.

DESIGN AND CHANCE

When I was at boarding school a succession of distinguished clerics came to preach to us in the chapel on Sunday mornings. They did their best to convince us of the existence of God and the truth of the Christian religion. Many of them attempted the same method of persuasion. They would begin by expanding on the marvels of modern science and the brilliant achievements of technology. We live in a wonderful world, they told us, and we should be proud to be growing up in the twentieth century with its ever-growing access to knowledge and practical skills in so many areas of life. At this point the preacher changed his tone. But, he said, and the 'but' was a signal that he was now going to say something religious – but, he said, there are many things that science cannot explain and which technology cannot do. Science cannot explain who God is or how he works. Technology cannot understand the mystery of life or create it in the laboratory. It is where human beings are ignorant and powerless, that is where God reigns. Even as a boy when I heard these eminent prelates I sensed the weakness of their arguments and was not convinced. If God is only to be found and his existence only to be proved in the blank spaces left by human ignorance and weakness, will not that space be constantly diminished as our knowledge grows and our capabilities are enhanced? Will not God eventually be squeezed out altogether? Of course, there are many things which are still beyond our understanding, and many achievements which are still beyond our abilities. But we can no longer rely on these gaps as a way of trying to persuade intelligent people that they should believe in God. Dr John Polkinghorne, the distinguished physicist, has written that the one god who is well and truly dead is the god of the gaps. 'The advance of scientific knowledge has given him a fading quality, so that he becomes a sort of divine Cheshire Cat.'[6]

Those who out of devotion to the God whom they worship are reluctant to take seriously the implications of modern science are frightened to take risks with their intelligence or imagination for fear of losing their faith. This reluctance to face up to the truth is, in itself, a lack of faith. It is far better to search for evidence in support of the existence of God by taking seriously the things we already know than to rely on ignorance to bolster up our faith. The scientist tries to make sense of the phenomena he studies. We do not have to worship that 'shadowy deity whose only role is to explain the currently inexplicable'. If some of the findings of science shake our faith and sow doubt, that is part of the necessary process demanded of those who are searching for the truth of the risk-taking God. Doubting raises the kind of questions which need to be asked if we are to move forward towards the next stage in our exploration into belief.

The Christian takes the findings of science seriously because he wants to know more about the world that God has created. To understand better what he has made is to understand better the mind of the Maker. But in our own time science has become increasingly complex. It describes the very large and the very small, things beyond our own experience. It talks about things which we cannot picture and which can only be described in mathematical and other symbols far beyond the grasp of those untrained in scientific discipline. At school I was told about molecules, atoms and electrons and believed that science had reached the core of the material world. Now when I try to read books on modern science – even those intended for laymen such as myself – I am baffled by the complexity of it all. Talk of protons, neutrons, quarks and gluons, of quantum physics, and of the simultaneous creation of time and space, leaves my head reeling. But enough penetrates my untrained imagination to glimpse, as from a far distance, the worlds which scientists today are exploring – the worlds of the unimaginably huge and of the unimaginably small. I am filled with wonder and exhilaration. I sense that when I stand up in church to say the creed and express my belief in God, creator of heaven and earth, I am attesting to a faith far more thrilling than when I first learned to say those words in my confirmation class sixty years ago.

From primitive times people have looked up at the skies, noted the regular movements of the sun, the moon and the stars, and wondered how it all began. In the familiar Genesis story God began his work of creation when 'the earth was a formless void and there was darkness over the deep'. In many other ancient myths there is a similar picture of chaos and formlessness out of which order came into being. An Assyrian account tells of the beginning 'when the sky had not been named and the earth was nameless and there existed only Apsu, the primordial ocean and Tiamet, the tumultuous sea'. Icelandic bards sang of the beginning of time when the earth did not exist, nor sky, a yawning abyss stretching through space. The Indian Hindu Vedas describes the time 'before being and not being, when there was a dark and watery chaos'. The Persian creation story recounts how the divine Ahura Nazoa spoke to the holy Zarathustra: 'I have created a universe where none existed', and the Greek poet Hesiod marks the beginning of creation by the arrival of Chaos and Chronos (Time). Haydn gave to the overture of his oratorio *The Creation* the title 'Representation of Chaos'.

In many cultures the relationship between chaos and order is a common theme in creation mythology. Mythology began to make way for science as the necessary tools for observation and measurement became available. Physicists, chemists and naturalists began to examine the matter with which the world is made and the function of living organisms. Their first conclusions led them to believe that creation was a wonderful and intricate mechanism which appeared to follow a logical programme laid down once upon a time by the Creator. It was only in the present century that theories began to be evolved which were to revolutionise earlier ideas about what happened 'in the beginning', and what has been happening in the universe ever since.

Today most scientists subscribe to the theory that the act of creation happened with what they nickname the Big Bang some time between ten and twenty thousand million years ago. At that moment all that ever was to be was in one 'place' described as infinitely dense and infinitely small. All the galaxies, all that was to be the stuff of continuing creation, was contained in the infinitesimal small spot when the Big Bang occurred. At that moment there was zero distance between all that would eventually become huge clusters of stars in space which was being created to contain them. From the moment of the Big Bang the galaxies have moved rapidly from the place where creation began and away from each other. They still move into space still being created. We live here on planet earth in a tiny part of a huge ever-expanding universe.

As if this does not stretch our imaginations enough, scientists now tell us that the Big Bang moment of creation was also the first moment of time and space. The logic of this is that we may no longer ask what was happening *before* the Big Bang. Time had not been created until that moment. Until that moment '*before*' had no meaning. Before that moment there was no space and therefore no happening. Because we are creatures of time and space we live on the assumption that everything has a prior cause. But before time and space existed there could be no prior cause. Most scientists (but not all) believe that the Big Bang hypothesis provides the best possible account of creation within the limits of our present knowledge, but behind the general theory many fascinating questions remain unanswered.

For example, hydrogen gas was once spread smoothly through-out space. It is a puzzle to know how it came to be gathered into 'lumps' to form galaxies. Questions such as this lead to fierce arguments among the experts to the bafflement of non-scientists who overhear their learned arguments. But with the bafflement comes a great sense of wonder and thrill at these hints about the way God must have worked in creation – and still works.[7]

From the moment of the Big Bang explosion the right chemi-cal components and physical circumstances were available to bring about the mind-boggling story. At first there was gas so hot that it glowed, expanding into space as it was created. The gas cooled forming infra-red and then radio waves. With lower and lower temperatures energy and matter were being continu-ally transformed into the first stars and galaxies. Elements were formed. Explosions created new galaxies. The incredible expanding universe was the womb waiting to give birth to exist-ence as we know it. Of this unfolding process much remains a mystery. And the process continues.

As we look back and try to imagine this great creative process over thousands of millions of years, we may detect the unfolding of purpose. Yet scientists have come to believe that purpose has only been achieved through a constant succession of chance events. The so-called 'uncertainty principle' in creation is one of the most remarkable findings of modern science and chal-lenges many of our traditional ideas about God. When the smallest particles which form the stuff of matter are studied, their behaviour seems to operate in such a random fashion that the immediate outcome is unpredictable. Far from following the mechanical pre-ordained sequence (like Paley's watch) they reveal a randomness which has been likened to throwing dice in which a number of possible results may follow. Eventually a sequence of chance events results in a viable pattern, but the pattern cannot be predicted in advance. Dr John Polkinghorne describes how this interplay of chance and necessity has charac-terised the evolution of the the universe, of living creatures and of the human race. We inhabit a world in which random events prove to be the originators of pattern.

Such a world is a world of orderliness, but not of clockwork regularity, of potentiality without predictability, endowed with an assurance of development but with a certain openness as to its exact form. It is inevitably a world with ragged edges, where order and disorder interlace each other and where the exploration of possibility by chance will lead not only to the evolution of systems of increasing complexity, endowed with new possibilities, but also to the evolution of systems imperfectly formed and malfunctioning. The former superior entities will earn the epithet 'successful' by their survival in the competition for constituent resources; the latter inferior entities will disappear from the evolving scene. It is just such a world as we live in.[8]

There can be a number of different ways of interpreting the role of chance in the evolutionary process. To some it is a clear indication that there can be no meaning in life. If the world and all that is in it is the product of innumerable random events, must we not agree with Macbeth that 'life is a tale told by an idiot, full of sound and fury, signifying nothing'? Although it was Einstein's own work on quantum mechanics that led to ideas of unpredictability and randomness, he found it hard to accept that the universe was governed by chance. He said that God does not play dice. But John Polkinghorne takes a more positive view:

Instead of seeing chance as an indication of the purposelessness and futility of the world, I was deeply moved by the thought of the astonishing fruitfulness in the inherent laws of atomic physics . . . the fact that they have such remarkable consequences as you and me speaks of the amazing potentiality contained in their structures. From this point of view the action of chance is to explore and realise that inherent fruitfulness.[9]

There seems to be a remarkable correlation between this understanding of the role of chance in the physical world, and the biblical view of the way that God reveals himself in the apparent random events of national and personal history.

THE UNFOLDING PROCESS

In 1687 Isaac Newton published his *Principia Mathematica*, one of the most influential books in the history of science. His analysis of the forces which cause the movements of the planets, including the earth with our moon, has profoundly influenced scientific work ever since, even though Einstein and others have now enlarged our vision further. In the same year that Newton published his masterpiece, the poet John Dryden wrote an ode in honour of St Cecilia, the patron saint of music. His view of creation was not with the analytical mind of a physicist but through the eyes of a poet. He likened the sequence of creation which led from the first beginnings to the flowering of Renaissance man as the unfolding of a great symphony.

> From harmony, from heavenly harmony
> This universal frame began:
> When nature underneath a heap
> Of jarring atoms lay . . .
> From harmony to harmony
> Through all the compass of the notes it ran,
> The diapason closing full in Man.

The events which led over thousands of millions of years from the earth as an immensely hot area of gas to a planet inhabited by human beings able to ask questions and find answers are gradually being pieced together by scientists. They reveal an astonishing story of how there must have been a period of a thousand million years between the time when the earth was sufficiently cool to allow the evolution of life and the actual moment when matter formed self-reproducing molecular systems to become living organisms. They reckon that life began two or three million years ago, with a huge period of time separating the creation of life from the Big Bang which initiated the whole process.

It is remarkable that it happened at all because this vital step of the appearance of life on our planet seems to have been subject to the same hit-and-miss random chance which we have already noted. Essential to the creation of life are the highly complex molecules called proteins which contain the necessary chemical ingredients. The chance of one such protein emerging out of the primitive stuff of creation is reckoned to be fifty million million million to one. In our own body cells there are two hundred thousand different proteins. The chance of life being created at all seems astronomical. Before it could happen, there must have been an immense sequence of possibilities, false starts, failures. The dice must have been thrown uncountable millions of times. The fact that I am writing this and you are reading it is mind-boggling when we consider how the dice must have been loaded against such an event happening at all. We are living evidence of a God who takes risks to achieve his purpose. As in physics, so biology shows that each stage in the evolution of living matter is reached through a complex series of random events. Looking back, with the benefit of hindsight, the story makes sense. But when each new stage was reached the outcome would have seemed unpredictable. Some might conclude that this development from the most primitive micro-organisms to intelligent human life was a matter of pure chance – the luck of the dice thrower. Others will want to give more weight to the meaning of the pattern which ultimately emerges from this huge succession of astonishing chances. Dr Arthur Peacocke sums up his view of the argument as an experienced biologist:

> Instead of being daunted by the role of chance in genetic mutations as the manifestation of irrationality in the universe, it would be more consistent with the observations to assert that the full gamut of the potentialities of living matter could only be explored through the agency of the rapid and frequent randomisation which is provided at the molecular level of DNA. The role of chance is what one would expect if the universe were so constructed that all the potential forms of organisation of matter (both living and non-living) which it contains might be explored. In principle, this is the only way in which all potentialities might eventually be given enough time and space to actualise.[10]

Human beings like to think that they have a special place in the order of creation, the crowning achievement of all that has gone before. This gives man a satisfying sense of his own importance in the universe, according him the liberty to do what he likes with the rest of the natural world. 'It is natural', wrote Francis Bacon, 'that man should be regarded the centre of the world, for if man ceased to exist the rest would be set adrift with neither aim nor plan.' The reported argument in 1868 between Bishop Samuel Wilberforce and Professor T. H. Huxley was less than edifying. The bishop asserted that the principle of natural selection was absolutely incompatible with the Word of God. 'If anyone were willing to trace his descent through an ape as his grandfather', the bishop asked, 'would he be equally willing to trace his descent on the side of his grandmother?' The scientist replied that he would prefer to be a descendant of a humble monkey than of a man who employs his knowledge and eloquence in misrepresenting those who are wearing out their lives in the search for the truth. There may seem to be a big evolutionary leap from chimpanzee to man, yet biology shows a continuous evolution. Human beings are made of the same stuff as the rest of creation. The story of creation is indivisible. God is involved in every moment of evolutionary process or he is involved in none of it. *Homo sapiens* emerged through the same creative process of hit-and-miss, chance and necessity, as has every other creature.

This is not the end of the story. The future is unknown. The work of creation continues. The universe continues to expand. New galaxies come into being. We are not living at the end of the earth's evolution unless we ourselves succeed in destroying it. We can only hazard a guess as to what the future holds for our planet. At the end of his television series, *Life on Earth*, David Attenborough dropped a tantalising hint. He confessed that in his comprehensive survey of the living creatures which inhabit our earth, he might have given the impression that man is the ultimate triumph of evolution and that all these thousands of millions of years had no other purpose than to put him on earth.

There is no scientific evidence whatsoever to support such a view and no reason to suppose that our stay here will be any more permanent than that of the dinosaur. The processes of evolution are still going on among plants and birds, insects and mammals. So it is more than likely that if men were to disappear from the face of the earth for whatever reason, there is a modest unobtrusive creature somewhere that would develop a new form and take our place.[11]

In this chapter we have taken a passing view of what modern scientists have to tell us about creation. The more we can discover how creation happens, the more we may be able to glimpse the character of the Creator himself. John Keble wrote in a hymn a quarter of a century before Charles Darwin published the *Origin of Species*:

> The works of God above, below,
> Within us and around,
> Are pages in the book, to show
> How God himself is found.

Advances in knowledge during the twentieth century have revealed the works of God to be more wonderful and more complex than Keble could ever have imagined. Bishop Jenkins of Durham was repeating Keble's vision when he wrote:

> To me it is absolutely spiritually and theologically clear that if you really believe that the God portrayed in the Bible is really the God of the whole of reality, then you must take modern world views absolutely seriously . . . The God of the Bible is not shut up in the Bible. He is at work in the world and it is in this actual contemporary world that he is at work.[12]

Science can neither prove nor disprove the existence of God. By revealing how creation happens it can give hints about the mind of the Maker. In an article in *The Times* discussing 'the rumour that physicists are on the verge of a theory capable of explaining everything about the universe', Russell Stannard, professor of physics at the Open University, asks whether God the Creator has been made redundant. He replies to his own question by claiming that the goal of a complete theory of everything is unattainable and that the claim to have disproved the need for a Creator is false. But this does not mean that we are now to go to the opposite extremes. 'Room for God? Yes. A knock-down proof of his existence? No. Granted that one applies the name God to whatever is the source and reason underlying the choice of physical laws, it still requires an act of faith to equate that source to the personal God of love and justice.'

What we can now learn about molecular and biological evolution presents us with a picture of a God who did not once upon a time perform a six-day job with a rest period on the seventh. He is an all-the-time creator, working continually in and through the processes which science describes. The evidence of random choice in the working out of that process opens up for us new concepts of a God who in the acts of creation leaves himself open for manoeuvre and exposes himself to risk. God is no longer to be seen as the clockmaker who, having once manufactured the mechanism and set it going, has now left his workshop to do another important job somewhere else. All the time he is at work within the process, taking risks to ensure the ultimate achievement of his purpose. John Polkinghorne, who is not only a distinguished physicist but also an ordained priest in the Church of England, brings together his scientific and theological insights when he writes:

> The actual balance between chance and necessity, contingency and potentiality which we perceive seems to me to be consistent with the will of a patient and subtle creator content to achieve his purpose through the unfolding of process and accepting thereby a measure of vulnerability and precariousness which also characterises the gift of freedom by love.[13]

Christians believe that this vulnerable and precarious God took the further risk of revealing himself within the time and space which he had himself created. He did this in the body of a human individual made of the same molecular and biological material as the rest of us. This astonishing fact does not contradict the evidence of science but carries it beyond the scope of biology and physics. Here, too, the elements of chance and randomness, contingency and potentiality, have their place.

4

CREED

WHEN WE SEARCH for the ratification of our faith and attempt to find suitable language in which to express it in a way appropriate to our own times, we find ourselves once again face to face with risk. It is at this point that those who count themselves to be committed Christians and those who can only claim to be on the fringe of belief and church membership begin to show signs of alarm. Has anyone the right to question the time-honoured words and phrases with which past generations were content to express their beliefs? This unease is well illustrated by Alan Bennett in his play *The Old Country*. His central character is a British spy who has defected to the Soviet Union and is living in self-imposed exile in a comfortable dacha on the outskirts of Moscow. From time to time news from the old country percolates through to him. He learns that English society is undergoing many changes since his defection, and he does not like what he hears. 'Is it true', he asks a British diplomat who is visiting him, 'that there are no longer Lyons teashops in London? Is it even true that the familiar words of the Authorised Version have been supplanted by a modern translation, and they have actually altered the creed?'

The majority of people in England seldom go to church except for occasional weddings and funerals, or on other special occasions. Yet they like to know that their local church is there as a stabilising factor in a changing society. When the Bible is translated into modern English, or the familiar cadences of the Book of Common Prayer's Order of Holy Communion gives way to something infelicitously called Rite A, or when bishops publicly cast doubt on the literal truth of some of the New Testament stories, there is widespread alarm. Agnostic professors of sociology and eminent literary figures write to the quality papers to deplore such threats to the national heritage. In a world at risk they expect the Church to be a symbol of the enduring things that cannot be shaken. Yet if the previous chapters are correct in their insistence that the God of the Bible and of science reveals himself as a risk-taking God, should not seekers after divine truth expect to encounter risk in their faith rather than fearing it?

THREE RISK-TAKING BISHOPS

Three twentieth-century bishops in the Church of England have set the cat among the pigeons because they have encouraged believers to take the dangerous path rather than to play safe. The first was Dr E. W. Barnes, Bishop of Birmingham, who in 1947 published a notorious book called *The Rise of Christianity*. His intention was to encourage his readers to reach for the truth as far as it could be ascertained. He was sceptical about the authority of the New Testament. He dismissed the miraculous element in the Gospel stories. He denied the literal historical truth of the virginal conception of Jesus and his bodily resurrection. He believed that traditional Christian doctrine could no longer be expected to appeal to educated men and women. Dr Barnes was a trained scientist, not a professional theologian or Bible scholar. Theologians reviewed the book savagely, doubting his competence to deal seriously with biblical and theological questions. What right had a scientist to pontificate on such matters, even if he had been made a bishop! The Archbishop of Canterbury, Dr Geoffrey Fisher, commented that if he had held these views he would feel that he could not hold episcopal office. The unrepentant bishop responded by repeating his ideas in more popular form in articles written for the mass-circulation *Sunday Pictorial*.

Sixteen years later, Bishop John Robinson of Woolwich created a much greater public sensation with *Honest to God*.[1] The provenance of this remarkable best-seller is well known. Bishop Mervyn Stockwood, in his autobiography, describes how he was aware of the risk he was taking when appointing John Robinson to be his suffragan bishop. John Robinson was, at that time, known in a limited circle as a good New Testament scholar and dean of a Cambridge college. It could not have been foreseen that he would become the author of one of the most sensational blockbusters in the history of religious publishing. Robinson was passionately concerned that the gospel should be presented intelligibly to the men and women of the 1960s to whom the traditional language and imagery of most preaching and religious writing made little sense. He had been inspired by the writings of such theologians as Paul Tillich and Dietrich Bonhoeffer who had set out to do just that. Was it to be his mission to make their thought even more available and understandable to the thousands of people who were consciously or unconsciously ready to receive the message of Jesus Christ if only it could be presented in a way relevant to their thinking and life experience? Forced to rest for some weeks with a back injury, Robinson crystallised his thoughts sufficiently to commit them to paper which he did in the space of a few weeks. The result was a modestly priced paper back of 141 pages. The first printing sold out on the day of publication, boosted by an article he himself had written on the previous Sunday for the *Observer* newspaper. The article was given the title 'Our Image of God must Go'. In the first year 300,000 copies were sold. Within three years, and after many reprints, the number had risen to over a million copies. It was translated into seventeen languages. There were many protests. The *Church Times* declared that it was not every day that a bishop goes on public record to deny almost every doctrine of the Church in which he holds office. Church officials and the press were deluged with letters accusing the bishop of heresy and demanding his resignation.

What was the reason for all this fuss created by what was undoubtedly, at that time, a risk-taking piece of episcopal writing? His main purpose was to 'come clean' and share with a wider public ideas which had been in common currency among theologians and many clergy for a long time. This thinking had liberated many of them from the shackles of traditional dogma and Robinson thought that it was his duty to allow others to have the same experience. In a chapter headed 'Reluctant Revolutions' he wrote: '. . . these questions must be explored. Or rather they are questions which are already being explored on many sides. The question is whether they remain on the fringes of intellectual debate, or are dragged into the middle and placed squarely under men's noses.'[2]

What are these questions? He asked whether we must continue to think of God as 'up there' or 'out there' in the way that the Greeks thought of their gods on the top of Mount Olympus. In reply, he popularised Bonhoeffer's concept of God as 'the ground of our being'. God does not intervene from outside, filling the gaps left by our impotence and ignorance. In denying the popular concept of God as a 'Daddy up in the sky' who is always there in the background, he risked shocking many of his readers by quoting with approval Bonhoeffer's celebrated (and often misunderstood) dictum that God is now teaching us that 'we must live as men who can get on very well without him'. He urged his readers to think of Jesus in a new way. Traditional ways of thinking almost inevitably suggested that Jesus was really God walking about on earth dressed up as a man; that he was not a human being born and bred as the rest of us are; that he was God for a limited time taking part in a charade; that he looked like a man, talked like a man, felt like a man, but underneath he was God dressed up – like Father Christmas. John Robinson was aware that this might be seen as an offensive parody, but he thought that it was perilously close to what most people were brought up to believe. He was at pains to emphasise the real humanity of Jesus and to minimise the supernatural and miraculous elements in the Gospel story. Jesus was a real man living totally in obedience to God and in love for others. In this way he was the unique revelation in history of what he called 'the human face of God'.

There was nothing innovative in all this. What was new was that it was being said in clear, non-technical language in easily available and inexpensive form. Reading it again after thirty years it is hard to see what all the fuss was about. It is now reckoned by many to be a quite conservative and slightly muddled statement of twentieth-century Christianity. But there is no doubt about the shock which *Honest to God* brought to the more traditional areas of Christian life in the 1960s, nor that this was a shock which was of lasting benefit to the Church. Since then it has been much easier to conduct sensible and honest theological discussion in the public domain, no longer to be confined behind closed doors. But that is not the end of the story. Twenty years later more shock waves were felt when Dr David Jenkins was appointed to the ancient and prestigious see of Durham.

Those who knew David Jenkins, had heard his lectures as a professor in Leeds University, or had read some of his books, cannot fail to have been surprised that a conservative Prime Minister should have recommended the appointment of a man well known for his radical views to a senior bishopric in the Church of England. It is not known whether Margaret Thatcher knew the man she had approved or whether subsequent events took her by surprise. In no way amongst the most radical of modern theologians, David Jenkins thinks it consistent with the teaching office of a bishop to be honest with the general public about his own questions and conclusions. In the pulpit, in the press and on radio and television he has expressed his convictions with courage if not always with clarity. Following in the footsteps of Barnes and Robinson he has had an even greater opportunity for making his views heard by a large popular audience. He has not been afraid of taking risks which have scandalised those clergy who have failed to keep abreast of contemporary biblical criticism and theological debate. In particular, his views on the virgin birth, miracles and the resurrection became the centre of vigorous controversy, though these matters had been subjects of urgent discussion in academic circles many years before Jenkins arrived in Durham. Many of the angry reactions have stemmed either from press reports taken out of context or from statements made 'off the cuff' in response to questions. There was a shocked response from many faithful laity who had been studiously shielded by their clergy from the contemporary debate on the assumption that these important matters should not be talked about 'in front of the children'. Subsequent debate has revealed that many lay men and women have been relieved to enter into these discussions and have sometimes shown a greater maturity than the clergy who tried to prevent them from doing so.

Bishop Jenkins has always been prepared to take risks for the sake of the gospel as he understands it and to which he is passionately committed. In his first Christmas letter to his diocese he wrote:

We have no right to insist on the literal truth of the story of the virgin birth of Jesus. To insist on literal language as a way of bearing witness to God is to get stuck into something very close to magic and superstition and to be in great danger of encouraging many unbelievers in the conviction that we religious people deal in fairy tales.

In his first Easter message he wrote at some length about his belief in the resurrection, about which he had earlier caused some offence by saying that what happened on the first Easter Day was more than 'a conjuring trick with bones'. He wrote:

I personally do not know whether the grave was empty or not. The evidence of the texts, the nature of tradition and the general facts about the way that people all over the world rapidly believe appropriate stories to support their religious beliefs, leave me wholly uncertain about the empty tomb as a literal historical fact.

Such public admission of episcopal uncertainty was not well received by those whose religious position gives them absolute certainty on basic matters of faith. Lord Hailsham said that Bishop Jenkins was undermining people's faith and Dr Graham Leonard, then Bishop of London, accused his fellow bishop of sowing doubt and confusion. Another diocesan bishop of evangelical persuasion suggested that Jenkins should resign his bishopric and return to academic work. The Church press was full of letters of protest, and anxious vicars sought to protect their flocks by assuring them that theologians were of the devil and simple believing Christians should not be led astray by them. Yet Bishop Jenkins makes the claim that of the thousands of letters he has received in the course of this controversy, the great majority have expressed agreement with his views, and their hope that the Church would provide more opportunities for discussing them.

There are obvious risks in the 'Durham approach', but it is clearly preferable to the common practice of ignoring his kind of views, or pretending that they have no significance for the proclamation of the gospel in today's world. A Church embarking on a decade of evangelism will lack credibility with a large section of the non-churchgoing public if it fails to face up positively and imaginatively to fundamental biblical and theological questions which require sensible and honest answers in the language not of yesterday but of today and tomorrow. Before his consecration, David Jenkins wrote of his concern for effective evangelism in a letter to the *Church Times*:

> Apostolic and missionary responsibility for the Christian faith demands, not the defence of credal formularies, but the exploration and exposition of the great Catholic symbols in the light of the best current knowledge and the deepest contemporary experience. The future of the Church lies with God's liveliness and not with our defensiveness. Nearly fifty years of conscious Christian discipleship, and well over thirty years of passionate study and teaching have convinced me that facing the issues of critical study, historical knowledge, and scientific thinking are essential to mission to our unbelieving and would-be believing fellows, as well as to the freedom and growth of our own Christian souls.

The fall-out from Dr Jenkins' public explosions had a profound effect on the Church of England, and beyond, in the 1980s. An examination of that fall-out may help us to understand more precisely the positive good which can come from daring to accept that the exploration and proclamation of the gospel is a risky business.

THE NATURE OF BELIEF

Church synods do not generally attract much public attention unless they are debating questions such as homosexual relations or the possibility of women becoming bishops. But when it became known that the 'Durham affair' was to be on the agenda of a forthcoming meeting of the Church of England General Synod, the media began to show considerable interest. They were hoping for a hot dispute between the Archbishop of Canterbury and a senior diocesan bishop. It did not happen in that way. When the debate took place in February 1985, Archbishop Runcie was in diplomatic mood. The Bishop of Durham sat silently throughout the four-hours debate, looking puzzled sometimes, smiling and nodding approval sometimes and occasionally making notes on his agenda paper. The focus of the discussion was on the biblical accounts of the virgin birth and resurrection of Christ. How could they be understood today? How essential was a literal acceptance of these events, as described in the New Testament, for the faith of the Church? The Archbishop of Canterbury spoke of the duty of bishops 'to banish and drive away all erroneous and strange opinions'. He had a conservative responsibility as a guarantor of historic continuity and a steward of apostolic faith. But the archbishop had no readiness for a heresy hunt. He spoke of the Anglican tradition of intellectual freedom and responsibility. The creeds remained profoundly important as guidelines and boundaries for the Church's thinking, embodying the accumulated wisdom of the Church's past in defining the limits of fruitful enquiry. But, he added, 'they do not preclude such enquiry; on the contrary, they are a stimulus to renewed attempts to interpret belief and its historic roots, in ways which intellectually, personally and pastorally satisfy. So a vigorous Church needs leadership which is a mixture of radical and conservative.'

Others were ready to take less eirenic lines, and to find the opportunity to attack the Bishop of Durham. From the 'high church' angle Bishop Graham Leonard accused Dr Jenkins of 'chipping away at the gospel to make it fit with a philosophy which is basically unbiblical'. The Revd David Holloway, a spokesman for evangelicals, was more precise: 'We have a cancer in the Church. In its early stages cancer is easy to deal with. But as it grows, it gradually strangles the whole.' Dr John Taylor, then Bishop of Winchester, would have none of this partisanship. His speech to the synod was a classic statement of the need to take risks if Christian dogma is not to stagnate. He pleaded with the synod to keep its balance and nerve and maintain the excellent middle way which was the special heritage of the Church of England.

> During the past decade I have seen the broad middle ground in all walks of life being eliminated. Extremists occupy the field, compromise is a term of abuse and confrontation is the order of the day. That is a recipe for self-

destruction in the nation and in the Church. Why has the discussion on the virgin birth and the resurrection, which goes no further than views expressed in the Doctrine Commission report forty years earlier, touched off such a strong reaction last summer? The cause must be partly in the deep insecurity and confusion of this generation. People everywhere look to their religion for a sense of certainty, order and meaning. But it helps nobody if they were to topple over into irrationality and merely stopped the mouths of those whose opinions were disturbing, or if they were to collude with the over-simplified half-truths which frightened people long to hear.

It was in response to the publicity given to this synod debate, with its conflicting views about basic Christian teaching, that the bishops felt obliged to work together to produce an agreed statement on the nature of Christian belief. They embarked on the difficult task of convincing the public that bishops of such varying views as Jenkins of Durham, Baughen of Chester and Leonard of London could honestly belong to the same ecclesiastical fold and proclaim the same creed. It was a tricky exercise in risk limitation, and it was not particularly successful. When it was published in 1986, it could not please everybody. Those in either the catholic or evangelical wings felt it was too much of a compromise with the liberals, fudging the dogmatic issues. Those of a more liberal disposition gave it a guarded welcome but criticised it for inconsistency and for dodging some of the more serious questions. The bishops claimed that it was a unanimous document, but it left the Church in very much the same position that it had been in before the Durham affair. This was, in fact, the best possible outcome. It was a classic example of having your cake and eating it. *The Nature of Christian Belief*[3] was in two sections – the Statement and the Exposition. The Statement, couched in traditional language, was designed to give the impression that Christianity was simply a matter of assenting to the authority of certain documents and formularies. These were summarised in a series of dogmatic propositions in the time-honoured language of traditional theology and used as a witness to the bishops' united adherence to the apostolic faith. They declared their belief that in Jesus Christ 'fully God and fully human, the Second Person of the Blessed Trinity is incarnate'. They upheld belief in 'the virginal conception as affirming that in Christ God has taken the initiative for our salvation by uniting with himself our human nature, so bringing to birth a new humanity'. They acknowledged belief 'that Christ's tomb was empty on the first Easter Day . . . as affirming that in the resurrection life the material order is redeemed and the fullness of human nature, bodily, mental and spiritual, is glorified for eternity'.

Far from solving the problems, statements of this kind leave wide open the questions which have been occupying the best theological minds for many decades. They will continue to perplex many thoughtful lay men and women who wonder what this kind of language means and what they are supposed to believe about it. Although the bishops may have satisfied themselves by agreeing to subscribe to this Statement, they knew that there are almost as many ways of interpreting what those words actually mean as there are episcopal sees! The Statement left the door slightly ajar by 'distinguishing in our teaching the ideas of theological exploration from the beliefs which are the corporate teachings of the Church'. But must not this 'theological exploration' be seen as an essential part of the 'corporate teaching' if dogma is not to stagnate? This dilemma is fortunately not entirely dodged. The second and more substantial part of the report was the Exposition which followed the Statement. What here was rightly exposed was that underneath the high-sounding language of dogmatic certainties, all the questions posed by the Bishop of Durham and many others remain unsolved.

Creeds presented a difficult problem, the bishops said in their Exposition:

> They are regarded as stating and defining rightly certain central beliefs which are found explicitly or implicitly in Scripture and have always been part of the living 'rule of faith of the Church'. In the creeds which we now acknowledge, the Church was led to conclusions on the true implications of Scripture which are not self-evidently the only possible ones . . . Commitment to the catholic creeds implies more than 'teachings agreeable to Scripture'. It

> means accepting as normative on specific points that inter-
> pretation of Scripture which the creeds authorise. The
> Church of England, therefore, in common with other
> credal Churches ascribes to the creeds as products of the
> Spirit-guided reflection, a limited but creative role in
> defining what is the faith which is uniquely revealed in
> Holy Scripture.[4]

This somewhat tortuous paragraph suggests that the bishops
had a difficult job in agreeing about the authority to be accorded
to the historic creeds. Almost every sentence raises an awkward
question. They state that the creeds 'define rightly certain central beliefs which are found explicitly or implicitly in Scripture'.
Certain beliefs? – who is to decide which beliefs among the
many which could be derived (implicitly or explicitly) from the
Bible are to be counted as necessary to faith?

The historic creeds were hammered out in the great Ecumenical Councils of the fourth and fifth centuries in an atmosphere which was often acrimonious and leading to violence.
Bishops were ready to anathematise one another, branding their
opponents as heretics and threatening excommunication or
worse. The careful language of the Nicene creed was born in the
conflicting atmosphere of power struggles in which theological
differences were mixed with ideological and nationalistic prejudices. For all their value it cannot be assumed that documents
forged to meet the needs of their own day will stand the test of
time unless they are continually reinterpreted in the thought
forms and the political, social, industrial and scientific presuppositions of succeeding generations. Every age must learn to grap-
ple with ancient truths within their contemporary context if the
truths inherited from the past, however valuable, are not to
fossilise and ultimately be rendered useless. The bishops recognised this when they wrote:

> This task of helping the world to know and understand the
> faith is a never-ending process. Where venerable words
> are still the best, yet they need to be explained in new ways
> to the children of new cultures. Where they are failing to
> communicate, new words have to be found to convey the
> original vision. Where new knowledge opens up a larger

and deeper conception of God, it has to be shown how the inheritance of faith is enriched and developed by this without losing its essential character. If this 'proclaiming afresh' is an exciting vocation, it is also an exacting one. At various periods it can be both painful and precarious.[5]

The bishops, having begun their response to the Jenkins business by affirming a number of clear dogmatic propositions, soon find themselves moving into an area of debate which forces them to acknowledge the riskiness of dogmatic definition. They remain cautious. They urge a spirit of discernment between what is authentic knowledge calling for new expression to match the enlargement of our insight into God, and what they describe as simply the current fashion which it is for the gospel to test and, if necessary, challenge. They recognise that crucial insights have been won by those who have the courage to question the faith.

Jesus promised his followers that the Holy Spirit would lead them into all truth. That promise will remain in the future tense until the end of time. At no point can either the Church or an individual Christian claim to have arrived at the place where there is nothing more to learn. In the life of faith exploration is a continuing process. Each arrival at new understanding is a signal for a fresh departure. Creeds are useful statements of how one group of people at one point in time understood the Christian faith. Their witness is of inestimable value to us, but they do not represent the end of our journey. That we must pursue for ourselves as others will do after us. In a valuable book on authority in the Roman Catholic Church, Hans Küng writes of those believers who 'have great concern for clear and unequivocal propositions, for the maximum possible definition of the official teaching of the Church, and for a system which would be as "closed" as possible.' This, he said, was characteristic of the first Vatican Council and in particular of the propositions of the Constitution of the Catholic Faith. 'Often when examining these positions one has the impression that one is looking at a photograph of a noble animal in motion, but caught by the photographer at an unlucky moment. Is this supposed to be our faith? is the question which arises.' He believed that

Vatican II presented a different picture, more relaxed and reflective of our times.

The work of many contemporary theologians performs this same service. But many credal statements and official formularies catch something of the awkwardness of Küng's unlucky animal.

> There is a difference between theology's striving for clarity in its propositions and claiming to have attained definitive clarity in those propositions. There is a difference between clearly indicating obscurities and difficulties, i.e., clearly stating what is unclear, and refusing to admit the existence of obscurities and difficulties and thus trying unclearly to push the unclear away. There is a difference between a theology that in all its struggle for truth remains always open for greater truth, and a theology that shuts truth and itself in the golden cage of a closed system.[6]

Faith in a risk-taking God will involve the recognition that any genuine exploration into his nature is certain to lead us out of our depth to where we have neither the language nor the imagery to express what is beyond our understanding. We know that we must be 'lost in wonder, love and praise'. For such explorers pious handbooks of devotion no longer satisfy, with their easy familiarity with the Almighty, and with the assumption that quick contact can be made with him by means of a celestial telex. Chatty prayers in divine worship are offered in language more suitable for a conversation with the postman or next-door neighbour. Such petitions can become embarrassingly inadequate when daring to approach the Immortal, Invisible, God only wise. 'God is infinite and incomprehensible', wrote John of Damascus (679–745), 'and all that is comprehensible about him is his infinity and incomprehensibility... God does not belong to the class of existing things: not that he has no existence, but that he is above all existing things, nay, even above existence itself.' Through the evidence of Scripture, through the life and teachings of Jesus Christ, through the testimony of saints, scholars and devout men and women all down the centuries, there is much that we can come to know about God. In prayer and meditation, Bible study and sacrament, we may even claim to have, in some way, access to him. Yet we are always only on the edge of understanding; it is always a matter of what T. S. Eliot called 'hints and guesses'. Beyond us, around us and within us is God the great Unknown. It is into this unknown territory that we take risks in the life of faith. The bishops with all their apparent certainties in their initial statement of faith, came to acknowledge the frontiers. Because God is what he is, the truth about him, however sympathetic to creatures made in his image, is bound to carry them beyond the limits of reason.

Those who hoped that the other bishops of the Church of England would be ganging up against the Bishop of Durham, solemnly declaring him a heretic, were disappointed. In presenting their report, *The Nature of Christian Belief*, Archbishop Runcie commended it as a consensus document and an affirmation of faith while leaving room for debate and argument: 'We have not thought it our duty to construct a barbed-wire entanglement, but have sought to affirm the articles of faith without excluding exploration.'

The report acknowledges that there must always be room in the Church for both tradition and enquiry. Diversity need not be a cause for division. Rightly understood it can become the means of deepening our understanding of the gospel and the way God works. But the bishops added a pious proviso. Diversity can only be permitted if 'we are attentive to the Holy Spirit as he glorifies Jesus and leads us into all truth'. This can quickly lead us into a Catch 22 situation. Part of the permitted diversity lies precisely in the many different and contradictory ways in which the guidance of the Holy Spirit is understood and claimed. The Holy Spirit can be (and is) frequently made the justification for any odd fancies we may want to uphold for ourselves or oppose in others. But one thing is certain, the Holy Spirit who Jesus said 'comes and goes in ways beyond our understanding' cannot be called upon simply to uphold venerable traditions. If he is the Spirit of the risk-taking God he will be seen as the Spirit of exploration leading into the necessity (to quote Karl Rahner) of 'going forward into a future ... of risk, of danger, and of hope in the incalculable grace of God'. Such risk-taking is an essential ingredient of a Spirit-led Church whose members, as St Paul wrote, 'never stop improving their knowledge and deepening their perception'.[7] This inevitably involves taking risks through trial and error, being willing to make mistakes, to live with contradictions, being prepared again and again for fresh starts, and to make the liberating discovery that conflict cannot always be avoided because it is part of the essential price to be paid for growth in understanding.

If risk is a necessary ingredient of faith, attempts to create uniform adherence to credal or catechetical statements or dogmas can be destructive of the very faith they are attempting to preserve. In 1971 a sharp debate arose in the synod of Roman Catholic bishops in Germany. Some members wished to have included on their agenda an open discussion on some of the more controversial theological and biblical questions such as the virginal conception, Christ's divine sonship and his bodily resurrection. Cardinal Höffner of Cologne ruled that such matters could have no place in an episcopal synod because those who denied them placed themselves outside the Catholic faith. How could they be a matter of debate in an assembly of bishops? One of the synod's consultants was the Jesuit theologian Karl Rahner. He argued that although these doctrines were unexceptionable, the forms in which they were generally expressed and taught were of little use to people today without the opportunity of further questioning and discussion. Rahner was concerned about the polarisation of theological and ecclesiastical issues and the unwillingness of people of differing viewpoints to listen seriously to one another:

> People are thoughtless and suspicious of each other; they label each other 'reactionary' or 'progressive': they attack each other, not with relevant arguments but with outbursts of feeling. Each group, each periodical, each newspaper, is simply given wholesale approval or wholesale condemnation. Someone who holds a different opinion is at once assumed by the other to be stupid or wicked, to be reactionary, or a modernist out to destroy Christianity. There are those who move only in circles which they feel instinctively to be sympathetic, without first examining them in a critical spirit. What is new is always accepted by some as the last word of supreme wisdom and by others as the greatest danger to Christianity of all time.

Rahner went on to argue that though it is quite reasonable for people in the Church to belong to groups of the like-minded, this must happen under certain clear conditions if the debate is not to become un-Christian and offensive:

> It is only when we have constantly and self-critically reminded ourselves that we, too, are and remain self-right-eous and narrow-minded people in such circumstances within the Church, and simply cannot exclude these shock-ing ingredients from our actions, that we may stand up as Christians for our opinions without this being at once depreciated as polarisation. Only then should we stand up boldly and militantly for our opinions, even though we know that the future never shows one 'party' to be wholly or solely in the right.[8]

Rahner's conclusion, and it is of great significance coming from one of the leading theologians of this century, is that each of us has to be liberated from a self-righteous and humourless fanaticism which we must not allow ourselves.

If pluralism is an essential factor in the Church of Jesus Christ, there are two alternative ways of dealing with it. It can either foster a conglomeration of opposing and seemingly irreconcilable camps, or it can promote understanding and unity by taking seriously the World Council of Churches' call to Christians to 'receive correction of one another in Christ'. A Church which consists of opposing factions turning deaf ears to one another is an immature Church. A maturing Church is one in which diversity is seen, not primarily as a problem to be solved but as a rich opportunity to be grasped for reaching out to new goals of understanding and mutual trust. This latter path is more risky and less safe than the former, but it leads to a greater enrichment of life.

CRUNCH QUESTIONS

So we come to the crunch questions. How can a Church include within its membership people of equal intelligence, integrity and spirituality who differ profoundly on such fundamental issues as the virginal conception of Jesus and his bodily resurrection? How can such divergent views be held together without destroying both the internal unity and the public credibility of the Church? Is 'correction of one another in Christ' a viable proposition across such wide chasms of belief and interpretation? Such questions might not have presented themselves to us if God had not taken the risk of revealing himself through events which claim to be rooted in history yet which are not immediately able to be verified historically. As the years went by legends and elaborations were added to the original memories of Jesus to give appropriate expression to the developing faith and experience of Christian believers. St Paul, writing his letters some thirty years after the death of Jesus, makes scant reference to the events of his life prior to the crucifixion. Does this mean that the historical facts which Matthew, Mark, Luke and John used to build up their story of Jesus of Nazareth are so unreliable, improbable or unimportant, that they can no longer be taken seriously as historical fact? In *The Nature of Christian Belief* the bishops take this question seriously. 'We are wrong', they insist, 'if we think that objective truths can only be conveyed by factual statements. Metaphor, poetry, symbolism may with equal validity express reality independently of the human mind. Certain truths are best conveyed in this way.' Yet, 'it must not be forgotten that Christian faith needs a sufficiency of historical facts to retain its traditional identity ... Legends only, however inspiring or profound, would prove a foundation of sand on which the fall could not be long delayed.' Following their own logic, and remaining true to the breadth of interpretation traditional in Anglicanism, they do not pursue more exactly what they intend by 'a sufficiency of historical facts'. They are keenly aware that many Christians hold that Scripture is inspired not only in its spiritual insights but also in the reliability of its historical statements. But they also affirm that it would be wrong to argue that all historical statements in the Bible must, as a matter of theoretical principle, be factually correct. The Church has no short cut or private road to historical certainty and there is nothing to lose but everything to gain from the responsible pursuit of historical criticism. Such typical manifestations of the Anglican temper may cause bewilderment in some minds, accusing the Church of 'woolliness' and 'fudging'. Why cannot it make up its mind whether the Bible is 'true' or not? It is the thesis of this present book that only by such apparent contradictions can the truth be pursued. This is how the risk-taking God sets about his self-revelation.

At the height of the controversy stirred up by Bishop Jenkins, the Archbishop of York, Dr John Habgood, wrote to *The Times*[9] hoping to clarify the debate. He drew attention to Karl Rahner's distinction between the *content* of faith and the grounds of faith. The two are related but not identical. The grounds of faith include a historical dimension which is characterised in Rahner's words by 'a certain element of uncertainty and ambiguity which is both inevitable and unsurmountable'. The content of faith, though substantially grounded in history, transcends its historical grounds. It is not a bare recital of events, but the recognition of certain events, stories, images and experiences as being revelatory of God. This recognition can have an immediacy and directness which is life-transforming. 'It is not', says Dr Habgood, 'always clear to discern the dividing line between revelatory events and revelatory stories, but within this general commitment to history, it is perfectly possible to accept that there may be Christian stories through which faith is conveyed and which remain valid for this purpose, but about which it is impossible to make historical judgements.'

It is essential to bear in mind this distinction between event and story when considering the two Gospel events which were the concern of the bishops when they met to examine the nature of belief. On the virginal conception they affirmed very strongly that those who accept the belief that Jesus was conceived in the womb of Mary by the creative power of the Holy Spirit without the intervention of a human father, can do so with full intellectual integrity. They can claim that they are holding fast to the teaching of the Universal Church as enshrined in the creeds. The event is described in Scripture, and there is no reason to believe that the evangelists invented the story. On the other hand those who find the historical evidence unsure see the story as told by Luke and Matthew as part of the nativity sequence which is generally accepted by scholars as legendary. The virginal conception is not mentioned elsewhere in the New Testament except in these two Gospels. In many ancient mythologies great heroes are said to have been conceived in some miraculous fashion, often as the result of intercourse between gods and humans. Archbishop Runcie told the General Synod that it was possible to believe in the incarnation while reserving judgement on specific historical points such as the virginal birth. 'Faith does not centre on negations and the absence of a human father. It was the action of God in uniting with himself our human nature, not the passivity of Joseph, which was central.' Bishop Jenkins made the same point in a Christmas message to his diocese: 'The birth narratives are far more about the obedience of Mary and Joseph in response to the unique graciousness of God than about Mary's physical virginity.'

By its very nature a definitive answer is impossible to ascertain about an intimate physical event which took place within the womb of Mary. No amount of historical research is likely to bring us any nearer to the truth of the matter. What matters in the end is not whether the story can be accepted as a historical fact but how (whether as an event or a story) it contributes to the building up of faith in God as revealed through Jesus Christ. It is here that both those who accept the tradition as stated in the creeds and those who question it, have much to gain from taking one another seriously. Those who hold tenaciously to the traditional beliefs do so because they want to bear witness to the uniqueness of Christ as Son of God. He was not just 'a very good man' or even 'the best man who ever lived'. He was a new creation, a second Adam, a fresh initiative of God on the human scene. In him the divine and human were perfectly fused. Conception in the womb of the virgin Mary provides a satisfactory explanation of how it happened.

Early Christian thinkers wondered how Jesus Christ could have been sinless when the rest of mankind conceived in the natural way inherited a proneness to sin as an inevitable consequence of their humanity. The story of the virginal conception provided a satisfactory *raison d'être* at a time when it was believed that life was transmitted solely through the male semen, the female womb acting merely as a nest in which the seminal child could develop. Sin was thought to be transmitted by the father through the sexual act. If Joseph had no part in the conception of Jesus the problem of his sinlessness could easily be explained. The bishops, without endorsing such an out-dated genetic theory, asked whether the child of human parents would not inevitably have shared in the imperfections of human nature. Would it not be difficult to believe that God would be able to live out his essential character of holy love in such a nature? Those who hold this traditional belief do so because they have a high doctrine of the uniqueness of Christ as the incarnate Son of God, a once-for-all event in history, demanding a once-for-all miracle to bring it about.

Those who wish to reject the literal story of the virgin birth do so not so much because they do not find the evidence convincing but because they wish to affirm the real humanity of Jesus who was, in the words of the Dutch theologian Edward Schillebeeckx, 'as human as we are, only more human'. They believe that God chose to reveal his absolute love for his creation in a human life lived under exactly the same conditions as we must live it. Like the rest of us, he was conceived by the sexual intercourse of a father and mother. Like us, he died a real death, as we all must. That God should reveal himself in this way, and act out his plan of salvation on the stage of human history, seems to them a far greater miracle than a divine intervention which sets aside the normal processes of human sexuality and conception which he himself as creator had ordained from the beginning.

It may seem strange that God who took such pains to reveal himself through the incarnation of his Son should have left the evidence of the way in which he was conceived in such an uncertain state. If he had intended us to know precisely how it happened, could he not have left some more exact information? It cannot be doubted that he *could* have done this. It is equally clear that he failed to do so. Yet is this not in character with the risk-taking God as we encounter him in Scripture and in science? It is as if he intended the way to faith to be not always along well-signposted roads but along routes where there are just enough hints and clues to invite exploration. Those who travel along this precarious road to faith need the courage to ask one another, 'What is the vision of God which comes to you through the beliefs that you hold?' and to have the patience and courage to wait for an answer. It is out of the very riskiness of uncertainty and exploration that there may come, through the process of mutual correction, a richer understanding of

Christ than if the reportage of sacred drama was so clear that
it allowed no discussion or meeting of minds.

'If Christ was not raised', wrote St Paul to the Christians in
Corinth, 'then our gospel is null and void, and so is your faith.'
At the heart of that faith is the credal statement that Jesus 'was
crucified for us under Pontius Pilate, suffered, was buried and
on the third day he rose again'. We have seen that it is possible
to discuss whether the virgin birth was an event or a story
without jeopardising our Christian faith. If the historical basis
for the resurrection is put similarly in doubt, is there a danger
of the whole edifice collapsing? We can dismiss any theories
that Jesus did not really die, or that his body was kidnapped
and resuscitated elsewhere. There is no reason to doubt Hans
Küng when he writes:

> His God-forsaken death may not be reinterpreted, turned
> into a mystery or myth as if it were only half true. Jesus's
> death was real, his abandonment by men and God obvious,
> his proclamation and his actions repudiated, his failure
> complete: a total break which death alone can achieve in
> the life and work of a man.[10]

Yet within a short time after that 'total break' there is clear
evidence from the contemporary letters of St Paul that men and
women were meeting together not to remember a good man
who had died, but to declare that Jesus is alive. What did this
mean? Even if Jesus actually foretold his rising again in the
hearing of his disciples (which many scholars think is doubtful)
there is a strong suggestion that they were very surprised when
it happened. As one of the characters in the Emmaus story put
it, 'Our hope had been that he would be the one to set Israel
free.' Yet already after the experience of Pentecost, Jesus was
the living centre of their lives, the ground of their new faith in
God, the living Lord who gave them the courage to face per-
secution and death, and the impetus to take their new faith with
fearless determination all over the known world. What happened
between Good Friday and Pentecost to account for such a
dramatic change in the lives of a number of seemingly ordinary
men and women? Whatever actually happened is what we call
the resurrection.

All four Gospels tell that the tomb was found empty on Easter morning. Obviously no one saw the body actually moving away, or disappearing, leaving behind the grave clothes. Eyewitnesses are reported to have claimed that they saw that this had happened. Yet the empty tomb is not mentioned in the earliest reference to the resurrection, and some scholars question whether this story was part of the first Christian proclamation. The New Testament scholar C. H. Dodd believed that when the evangelists came to write their accounts of the resurrection they had on their hands a solid piece of tradition about the empty tomb which they were bound to respect 'though it did not add much cogency to their message and they hardly knew what to make of it.' The Bishop of Durham also prefers to leave the question open: 'I cannot cheat or conceal on this because the matter is too important and God is too clearly Truth for cheating or concealment or pretending to particular beliefs that one does not find sufficient reason for believing. In any case, the empty tomb cannot prove, does not establish and may not even mean resurrection.'

The empty tomb is not the most important evidence which the New Testament presents in support of the resurrection faith. When the Gospels came to be written the evangelists were able to choose from a number of stories of resurrection appearances then in circulation. It is not easy to piece them together to make a logical sequence. The figure of Jesus is mysterious. He can be touched. He breaks bread. He breathes, walks and talks. Yet he arrives through closed doors, is not always recognisable and vanishes at will. Are these historical events or theological stories – or half way between the two? Dr J. K. Elliott of the department of theology in Leeds University speaks of them as 'faith legends': 'The likely origin of these stories is that the earliest believers did indeed claim to have seen Jesus even if we speak of their experiences as subjective visions. What the evangelists do is to dramatise these visions and make them objective.' The Church of England bishops, while recognising that the divergent opinions evident among scholars are reflected among themselves, nevertheless wished to be more specific: '. . . the mode of existence of the Risen Lord was one in which his full human nature and identity, bodily, mental and spiritual was present and glorified in eternal blessedness; that this mode of existence was observed and experienced and its essential secret grasped by numbers of his disciples in personal encounter'. In our experience here on earth bodily and mental processes are determined by the laws of physics and chemistry. What exactly the bishops meant when they said that human faculties of body and mind, which we can only understand within our time and space dimension, are 'glorified in eternal blessedness' is not at all clear. St Paul found himself in great difficulties when he tried to explain the resurrection of the body.

All profound theological questions lead into mystery beyond the capacity of logical language. They demand a humble and reticent agnosticism. After David Jenkins had stirred up controversy about the resurrection, Bishop Tinsley, formerly of Bristol, wrote in his diocesan leaflet to give sound advice to his flock. He told them that the 'thing itself – Christ's resurrection – is completely intangible and unimaginable. It can only be expressed in pictorial graphic expressions, metaphors, images and symbols. It is often hard for the human mind to live patiently with symbols and with parables since we prefer proofs, guaranteed certainties to our own prescription of what certainty is. But that would be for God to impose himself in a way that would infringe our genuine and free personalities.'

Here is the strange paradox of the risk-taking God who has so ordered the evidence which bears witness to the supreme event in human history – the resurrection of Christ – that men and women can interpret it in many different ways in their search for the truth which should eventually bring them together. For some, faith in the Risen Lord springs from a firm belief in the empty tomb, the objective physical appearances to the disciples and the bodily ascension into heaven. For others, the resurrection faith gains in power, wonder and meaning when the supernatural 'magical' element in the story is played down, and the drama of redemption is seen to be acted out on the human scene within the natural context of time and space. To those who hold the first view encouragement comes from the accounts of the disciples entering into the tomb, 'seeing and believing'. To those who hold the second view, reassurance comes from the words spoken to doubting Thomas, 'Happy are those who have not seen and yet believe.'

We must take seriously the variety of God's gifts of intelligence, imagination and faith which he has distributed among us. We must also take one another seriously if 'correction of one another in Christ' is not to degenerate into easy compromise, facile tolerance or ill-disguised hostility. The risk-taking God has revealed himself in the Bible, in creation and in Jesus Christ in such a way that there must be wide-open possibilities of interpretation and understanding of his purpose for us. How else can individual minds, isolated from one another, begin to glimpse the majesty and providence of God who is, on any account, beyond our understanding? It is not by a monochrome faith but by the rich diversity of approaches in which all are able to engage with one another creatively, that there is any possibility of growth in knowledge of God and obedience to him.

In the debate on doctrine in the General Synod of the summer of 1986, Dr Robert Runcie showed himself to be a wise and moderating leader. He said:

> We are confident that the Church is enriched when our feet are set on a path broad enough for us to move forward with freedom and integrity. We need to respect one another's right to occupy such a path. We need to be patient and sensitive with one another's difficulties. We grow in freedom.

It is the God who takes risks who invites us to dig deeply as we explore together the revelation of himself given to us through Jesus Christ who was born on earth from Mary, lived and died in Palestine, and rose from the dead.

5

AUTHORITY

CRISIS OF AUTHORITY

JESUS MADE a deep impression on his contemporaries because 'he taught them with authority and not like their own scribes'. The Roman army officer who asked him to heal one of his servants who was dying, backed up his request by explaining that his job had taught him to recognise authority when he saw it. For the Christian the words and deeds of Jesus have a unique authority. Preachers daringly assume that authority when they stand in their pulpits and declare that what they are about to utter is given 'in the name of God'. Is such an ascription the truth or an outrageous effrontery?

In the previous chapter it was noted that church leaders and ecclesiastical synods are capable of making contradictory statements on almost every aspect of Christian faith and life. This is a risk that God is prepared to take with his Church. Yet the evidence of recent statistics suggests that it is those churches which present an authoritative message which are increasing in numbers. It is the middle-of-the-road congregations which are on the decline in many places. Is a conservative Pope who strongly upholds traditional doctrines of faith and order or the biblical fundamentalist who proclaims the absolute authority of Scripture a more powerful witness to the faith today than those whose approach is more tentative because when they meet contradictions they are ready to try to understand both sides of the argument? Is the era of the risk-taking God passing away in favour of a Divine Dictator?

The second half of the twentieth century has been marked by a challenge to old concepts of authority in every aspect of life. It has affected politics, the family, public and private morality, education and much else. The Church has not been immune from this disturbance. Doubt is cast on the authority which bishops and clergy claim to have by virtue of their office. Doubt is cast on the wisdom of ecclesiastical synods. Doubt is cast on the traditional authority accorded to the Bible, the creeds and pronouncements by the Church itself. The right of individual conscience to stand out against official declarations of Church and state finds daily expression in acts of ecclesiastical and civil disobedience.

Some people profoundly regret this decline of respect for lawful authority which it is said was once taken for granted in the Church. Others see it as a welcome sign of a Church 'coming of age' and beginning to discover what St Paul called 'the glorious liberty of the children of God'. After the publication of the controversial papal encyclical *Humanae Vitae*, thirty Roman Catholic priests wrote in a letter to *The Times*, 'One listens with respect to the Holy Father, but we are not expected to renounce our will to think for ourselves.' At a time when many priests were questioning papal and episcopal authority, Monsignor Derek Warlock chose to speak in his installation as Archbishop of Liverpool on the concept of the bishop as a father in God. In family life the authority of the father changes from one generation to another. He asked what concept of fatherhood was appropriate for a bishop today. Addressing the synod of Roman Catholic bishops in Germany, Karl Rahner remarked that although a pastor should remain a pastor, 'this certainly does not mean that he should treat his flock as if they really were sheep.'

The problems facing the Church and secular society are much the same when the subject of authority is under discussion. How can discipline necessary for the maintenance of the common good be maintained without creating paralysis? 'Whenever people say "Let us be free" ', the composer Karl-Heinz Stockhausen once wrote, 'it produces chaos and destruction because they have never learned to use freedom as a means of restricting oneself so that others may be free.' Although the Bible talks about perfect freedom being achieved by serving God, the Church has never found it easy to determine the relationship between authority and freedom in its own life. Throughout its history ecclesiastical harmony has been bedevilled by this problem. God seems to have taken a great risk in creating the Church as his instrument for the fulfilment of his purpose and failing to give very clear instructions about the basis of authority upon which its life and work must be founded. This is the area of debate which creates some of the toughest problems for the ecumenical movement.

Every Christian tradition in one way or another claims that it derives its ultimate authority for its teaching and ordering from Holy Scripture. Anglicans claim that the Bible 'contains all things necessary for salvation'. But who is to interpret the Bible and decide what parts of the Scripture are compulsory for belief, and what parts might be considered optional or even ignored? Soon after his appointment to Canterbury, Dr George Carey was asked about his attitude to the Bible. 'I have always been a gospel-centred person', he replied, 'but I could never be a narrow person . . . I would want to say that the people with the highest doctrine of Scripture, namely the evangelicals, do not treat the Bible with the respect that the liberals do. They do not analyse it in the depth it calls for.' Does this mean that the authority of the Bible as a guide to Christian belief and action depends on the individual's capacity to 'analyse it in depth'? Obviously the archbishop did not intend to suggest that a first class degree in biblical studies is a necessary qualification for salvation. But he was making an important point. The Bible is not an easy collection of writings to understand. It does not work by magic. 'How can I understand unless someone gives me a clue?' the Ethiopian asked Philip as he was trying to make sense of a passage in Isaiah. The question remains. Who is the necessary 'someone'? How is the clue to be given?

The Anglican-Roman Catholic International Commission (ARCIC) discussed this question in its final report. The inspired documents of Scripture containing the words and deeds of Jesus, the saving activity of God, came to be accepted by the Church as the normative record of the authentic foundations of the faith.

> To these the Church has recourse for the inspiration of its life and mission; to these the Church refers its teaching and practice. Through these written words the authority of the Word of God is conveyed. Entrusted with these

documents the Christian community is enabled by the Holy Spirit to live out the Gospel and so to be led into all truth.[1]

This is an unexceptional statement. Yet once we start employing phrases such as 'being led into all truth by the Holy Spirit' we find ourselves walking on slippery ground. 'Being led' is the language of process. It suggests provisionality. There is always more to be revealed. We have never reached the whole truth. So we must be cautious of precise or absolutist definitions. We find ourselves again in a Catch 22 situation. If our understanding of the Bible is to be tested by the Holy Spirit, is our understanding of the Holy Spirit to be tested by the Bible? In his advice to the German bishops, Karl Rahner spoke about preaching:

> A preacher should pray for the grace of existential imagination so that he can really preach in the way that is necessary today; slowly, cautiously, gently, groping step by step towards that reality for which he had hitherto always been ready with too many words; modestly and even disturbed as he realises how difficult it is to attest real faith and not merely its historical and social objectivations and relics. Don't try to console when there is no scope for consolation. Don't 'solve' life's problems when their sole ultimate solution lies in God's incomprehensibility, his nature and his freedom.[2]

Such an admission of provisionality and uncertainty from a distinguished Jesuit theologian may shock the fundamentalist who, Bible in hand, declares it to be the authentic and unambiguous Word of God. It may equally alarm the local Catholic (Roman or Anglican) who steadfastly holds in veneration (with Cardinal Newman) 'Holy Church as God's creation, and her teachings as his own'. Yet however much we long for, and others demand of us, a clear, authentic, authoritative message about God and his purpose for humanity, we have to be honest and confess with St Paul that while we are here on earth we can see things only as a 'dim reflection in a mirror'. This is the way the risk-taking God tests our faith in him. It is the way of courageous exploration not of precise definition.

True as this is, the Church is not just a movement of like-minded well-wishers seeking after faith – an informal club for the religiously minded. It is an institution, and institutions need structures. Structures need guidelines for belief and policy if they are not to disintegrate. In the prevailing distrust of authoritarianism Church structures are under threat. Biblical fundamentalism is fighting a rearguard action against biblical scholarship and new scientific knowledge. Roman Catholic and Anglican concepts of authority in the Church are also threatened. God is demanding that each of these communions should take risks to enable them to move effectively into the future.

MAGISTERIUM

Addressing a group of Brazilian bishops in the Vatican in February 1990, Pope John Paul II told them that it would be an inversion of values to subordinate the authority of the bishop to human choice. 'The authority of the bishop requires ratification from no human quarters,' he told them. The task of a bishop is 'to sanctify, instruct, and govern the people of God'. This is a ministry that 'only the successors of the apostles receive from Christ which they exercise in his name'. As the biblical fundamentalist attempts to reject or minimise the scholarly criticism of Scripture, so the Pope has been particularly concerned to ensure that the bishops resist any liberal tendencies which he sees as giving way to 'worldliness'. To fall into the 'modernist trap' is to betray Jesus Christ with whom the episcopacy has 'an original and irreversible relationship'. The people of God have a duty to listen to Jesus Christ through the bishops who receive from him not the words of men but the Word of God.

In May 1980 the Roman Catholic bishops of England and Wales called together a National Pastoral Congress to meet in Liverpool. It had been well prepared under the leadership of Archbishop Derek Warlock in the spirit of the Second Vatican Council. For the long weekend of Pentecost the bishops met with nearly two thousand clergy, religious and laity, chosen to represent every section of the Roman Catholic Church. There was a remarkable openness in the discussion, particularly on the part of the laity. The radical voice was allowed to be heard with the urgent request to the hierarchy to give serious consideration to such burning issues as ecumenism, intercommunion, contraception, the ordination of women to the priesthood, the marriage of priests, and in particular to the granting of a greater role to the laity in the decision-making councils of the Church. Within two months a report was published in the shape of a Message from the bishops giving their response to all that was said and done at the Congress.

For the non-Roman Catholic reader there is particular value in the sections on evangelism, the nature of the Church, the Mass, the poor, and peace and justice. After twelve years the document remains an important guide to Roman Catholic thinking in England and Wales on key issues at the end of the twentieth century. No less interesting, though in an ecumenical context more controversial, is the way in which the bishops used the Message to stress the importance of obedience to their own authority. They reported that they were struck by the way bishops, clergy and laity 'trusted each other, listened to each other as each had something valuable to contribute'. But it is obvious that the wide-ranging and critical comments of the laity reinforced the bishops in their belief in their own *magisterium*. In parts of the Message the bishops seem to suggest that the main purpose of the Pastoral Congress was to stress the importance of their episcopal status and to reinforce their authority. A key passage states:

> By virtue of our episcopal consecration and in the light of the spirit and teaching of the great Council (Vatican II) we the bishops of England and Wales, as vicars of Christ in our dioceses, have the duty and the right to preach the Gospel to our people in season and out of season, and always in communion with our fellow bishops and especially the Bishop of Rome. We have the duty and the right to call upon all priests and people alike for a loyal and respectful acceptance of our teaching.[3]

As if to discourage criticism of their authority, the bishops made plain that the Church must not be seen either as a centre of higher studies or as a debating society. It is much more like a family than a political society. But even in a family bound together by love and mutual acceptance, some structures and forms of authority are needed, and decisions taken for the sake of the family. The bishop is father of the family which is his diocese. But there was a hint that the definition of episcopal fatherhood was more akin to the *paterfamilias* of a Victorian family who 'lays down the law' than in a modern democratic family in which each member from the oldest to the youngest has some share in decision making:

> The universal episcopate can, in matters of supreme importance, exercise its teaching authority function, its *magisterium*, by an infallible definition of some point of revealed truth. The same is true of the Pope as head of the college of bishops.[4]

Many loyal Roman Catholics, seeing what appears to be chaos reigning in other denominations, are grateful for the clear and authoritative leads which the *magisterium* provides for their Church. How else could unity be maintained in so huge a body as the world-wide Roman Catholic Church? The strong claim by the episcopate to their God-given authority comes as a powerful reassurance of stability in a changing world. They have no wish to have risks taken with them which might strain their loyalty to the tradition of their fathers. But some representatives at the Liverpool congress were disturbed that some serious questions which they raised at the meetings were brushed aside by the bishops with scant notice being taken of their requests. Are policies regarding the ordination of women to the priesthood, the marriage of priests, intercommunion, and contraception so cut-and-dried that open discussion on such issues must be discouraged or even disallowed? Are not these precisely the questions upon which the laity have a particular competence to make decisions, with more actual relevant experience than their bishops or priests? Must the Church forever remain a body which is ruled by a minority who are the paid officials, without any assistance from the laity who represent the vast majority of the membership? As some of the lay representatives remarked after Congress, although there was much flattering talk about the great contribution the laity have to make to the Church, this was not matched by giving them any real responsibility where the actual decisions which concern them most are made. This lay pressure caused the bishops to send up alarm signals in the Message in response to the call that had been heard from some people asking for greater democracy in the Church.

> To be numbered among God's people should confer on each baptised individual a sense of belonging and personal identity, of dignity and purpose. It also confers on each a fundamental equality and a shared vocation to worship and work together in society in a collaboration which befits God's people. This is in no sense a democratisation, nor is it a refusal to acknowledge differences of graces, gifts, functions and ministries within a hierarchical Church.[5]

In recent years in Britain and elsewhere the Roman Catholic Church has taken considerable steps forward in giving laity a greater part in the worship and witness of parochial life. Priests are encouraged to discover the depths of their own vocation by active and lively collaboration with lay people. They are told that they need the help of the laity to make their own priestly ministry more effective, just as the laity should expect their priests to set the problems they have to face in their daily lives in the context of the gospel. But even the contemplation of a partnership between priest and layman raises anxieties about the dangers of democracy. 'True collaboration does not blur distinctions between ministries. It clarifies the distinction and shows the ministries to be complementary in the life and mission of the family of the Church.'[6] Priests are to remain a race apart.

Despite these hierarchical fears, Karl Rahner urged that there should be a gradual process of democratisation to prepare for the Church of the future. He suggested that this should begin with a more democratic method of appointing ecclesiastical officers. It is, he said, hard to see why at least the priests of the diocese concerned should not co-operate really effectively in the election of their bishop. Also, 'is not a more obvious participation of the laity required, not only in the appointment of office holders but in other decision-making processes in the life of the Church?' He said:

> In such decisions it must be admitted that the bishop has a personal and inalienable right which is qualitatively

different from any existing or conceivable right of other members of the Church to share in discussion, but this does not mean at all that priests and lay people can never have more than advisory functions in regard to these decisions.[7]

Dom Bede Griffiths has suggested that together with the *magisterium* (the Pope and the bishops), there are two other organs of authority which need to be employed – the laity and the theologians. We have already seen that the laity are welcomed as collaborators both in the liturgy and in some aspects of parochial life as long as they do not ask for democratic authority. To those who already enjoy authority, democratic sharing seems too great a risk. But in recent years the theologians have faced the *magisterium* with an even more embarrassing challenge.

THEOLOGIANS AT RISK

Conservative evangelicals are suspicious of theologians lest they shake the faith of simple believers. The Vatican is equally critical of them for fear that they undermine the official authority of the Church. From both sources theologians are suspect because they invite the faithful to take risks with their faith. But each new generation of Christians needs theologians to prevent the Church from succumbing to inertia. The second Vatican Council, summoned by Pope John XXIII in 1962, served as a remarkable catalyst to the Roman Catholic Church which was in need of a shake-up. It has been compared with Gorbachev's policies of *glasnost* and *perestroika* which were to have such a profound effect on the nations of Eastern Europe and on the Soviet Union itself. Vatican II brought about speedy changes in liturgical practice, in the involvement of the laity and in new ecumenical concern. It also gave encouragement to a number of distinguished Roman Catholic theologians, such as Karl Rahner, Hans Küng and Edward Schillebeeckx who increasingly attracted attention by their writings and lectures, not only in their academic circles, but in the Roman Catholic Church and beyond. They had themselves made a considerable contribution to the thought of Vatican II and the new spirit in the Church

which it stimulated. There was a wide welcome for new opportunities for reading and discussing the great theological and
ethical questions of the day with honesty and clarity.

Before Vatican II had ended its deliberations, Pope John
XXIII was dead. Under his successor Paul VI many of the
Council's reforms were speedily implemented and widely welcomed. But among the more conservative leaders there was fear
that these reforms were going too far and too fast. When John
Paul II succeeded to the papacy in 1978 it soon became clear
that a man of different temper was now in charge. In spite of
his charismatic and attractive personality he was at heart a
traditionalist. He believed that the time had come to apply the
brakes. This he set out to do in homilies and addresses delivered
in the course of his world-wide travels. He suspected the liberal
tendencies of many of the best-known theologians and discouraged priestly political activism, particularly in South America.
Wherever possible, bishops of a radical frame of mind were
succeeded by those who were more traditional. The Vatican
was moving towards a headlong collision with some of the most
notable theologians. Some had already been called to account
and threatened with disciplinary action for their alleged hetero-
doxy.

As early as 1969, some 163 professors of theology signed
what came to be called the Cologne Declaration 'for the freedom
of theology and theologians'. In course of time many more
academic signatures were added to the document which
received wide publicity. It stated that, while upholding and
affirming the teaching office (*magisterium*) of the Pope and
bishops:

> We know that this pastoral office cannot and must not
> supersede, hamper and impede the teaching task of the
> theologians and scholars. Any form of inquisition, however
> subtle, not only harms the development of sound theology;
> it also causes irreparable damage to the credibility of the
> Church as a community in the modern world.

Expressing the hope that the Pope and the bishops would trust
the theologians as a matter of course, and support without any
prejudice their work as theologians for the welfare and well-
being of mankind in the Church and the world, they added:

We would like to fulfill our duty which is to seek the truth and speak the truth without being hampered by administrative measures and sanctions. We expect our freedom to be respected whenever we pronounce or publish, to the best of our knowledge and in conscience, our well found theological convictions.

Two years after the Cologne Declaration one of its signatories, Hans Küng, professor of dogmatic theology in the university of Tübingen, published his book *Infallibility? An Enquiry*. As the question mark in the title made clear, the work was strongly critical of the dogma of papal infallibility and the authoritarian stance of the *magisterium*. It was not long before his licence as an accredited Catholic teacher was withdrawn. Undeterred by his Church's official ban, he travelled widely, wrote a series of best-selling theological books, and continued to attract large numbers to his lectures in the university and elsewhere. In a newspaper article marking the tenth anniversary of the withdrawal of his official teaching licence, he declared that the Vatican strategy had quite clearly been to shunt him to one side in the university, isolate him from the Church, and make him as uninteresting as possible. But far from becoming a 'theological wallflower', he claimed that his lectures were now more enthusiastically attended and his books more widely circulated among Roman Catholics than ever before. The steps taken against him, he said, were theologically unwarranted, legally unjustified and counter-productive. He hit back at the Vatican, describing it as Europe's last absolutist state, an *ancien régime* that may publicly demand human rights from others, but in its own sphere gags the freedom of conscience, of the press and of opinion. Küng recognised that bishops, committed to their teaching office, were caught in the middle of a hopeless situation because 'they are trained, selected and sworn to carry out without question the orders of the Roman authorities and to denounce possible opponents'. But, he added, at least clergy and laity are rebelling and seeking a different course. Among the laymen who chose to rebel was the novelist Graham Greene, who said that the Roman Curia reminded him a bit of the *Politburo*, adding a little wistfully that even the *Politburo* was changing.[8] Hans Küng's statement, and those of other distinguished academics, sparked off a debate on the nature of authority in the Roman Catholic Church which will not quickly subside.

In the summer of 1990 the Vatican retaliated with a document prepared by the Congregation of the Doctrine of Faith, once known as the Holy Inquisition. It issued what it called an Instruction on the relationship between the teaching office of the Church (*magisterium*) and the work of the theologians. Thousands of theologians hold academic posts under ecclesiastical control and many of them are unwilling to endorse the strict 'party line' on theological and ethical questions. 'The purpose of God for his people', says the Instruction, 'is to free them from the snare of the father of lies.' Because the *magisterium* is convinced that some theologians have become so ensnared, it declares that it has the responsibility to set strict limitations on their freedom to operate. The theologian is not to see himself as an independent explorer after truth, but as a servant of the *magisterium*. 'His role is to pursue a particular way of ever deeper understanding of the Word of God found in the inspired Scriptures and handed on by the living tradition of the Church. He does this in communion with the *magisterium* which has been charged with the responsibility of preserving the deposit of faith.' In other words, the theologian must recognise that both his methodology and his conclusions are already circumscribed. Theologians are warned against evaluating the truths given through divine revelation by subjecting them to the judgement of other academic disciplines. They must remember that 'the ultimate normative principle for such discernment is revealed doctrine which itself must furnish the criteria for the evaluation of the elements and conceptual tools, and not vice-versa.'

Again and again the Instruction makes clear to the theologians that the *magisterium* is 'the sole authentic interpreter of the Word of God, written and handed down by virtue of the authority it exercises in the name of Christ'. Absolute weight must be given to its statements because Christ has bestowed upon the pastors of the Church the 'charism of infallibility in matters of faith and morals'. The Instruction was concerned to widen the scope of infallibility beyond the normal confines of the infallible declarations of ecumenical councils and *ex cathedra* decrees of the Pope. It speaks of pronouncements which are concerned with 'some teaching which leads to a better understanding of Revelation in matters of faith and to moral directives derived from such teaching.' In addition, the Instruction makes clear that in matters of discipline, magisterial decisions, even if they are not guaranteed by the charism of infallibility, and are therefore reformable, are 'not without divine assistance and therefore call for the adherence of the faithful'. From this it is concluded that even if the pronouncements of the *magisterium* in the past contained deficiencies, their pronouncements were justified at the time. The logic of this is that even if today some decree of the *magisterium* may be found deficient and therefore reformable, the divine assistance accorded to the Roman authority requires the faithful to accept them as requiring consent and obedience. Commenting on these provisions, a French Dominican theologian exclaimed, 'The Curia sews it up.' Theologians have been left little room for manoeuvre.

What advice does the Instruction give to those theologians who in all conscience cannot accept the strait-jacket into which their responsible academic work is placed by these regulations? It acknowledges that even when collaboration takes place between the bishops and the theologians under the most favourable conditions, the possibility of tensions between them cannot be ruled out. 'If tensions do not spring from hostile and contrary feelings, they can become a dynamic factor, a stimulus to both the *magisterium* and the theologians to fulfil their respective roles while practising dialogue.' But when all is said and done, the theologian is not permitted to follow his conscience because difficulties in accepting magisterial teaching cannot be justified: 'Conscience does not constitute an autonomous and exclusive authority for deciding the truth of a doctrine.'

If the theologian continues to find himself at odds with the teaching of the *magisterium*, what should he then do? The Instruction tells him that he must first give intense and patient reflection, to be ready to revise his own opinions, and listen to any objections his colleagues might offer to him. If his difficulties persist, he has a positive duty to make his problems known to the magisterial authorities 'in an evangelical spirit and with a profound desire to resolve the difficulties'. He must, in the meantime, avoid turning to the mass media and refrain from giving 'untimely public expression to divergent opinions'. He should not associate himself with pressure groups which attempt to promote parallel magisterial bodies. Whatever reservations he has about official teaching, he should keep them privately to himself. He is told that he needs discernment as well as a true mastery of the issues involved. He must not lose, by conforming himself to the present world, the independence of judgement which is that of a disciple of Christ. If finally the *magisterium* is led to believe that the work of a theologian is a threat to sound doctrine and a stumbling block to the faithful, it can at times be led to take serious measures as, for example, when it withdraws the canonical mission and teaching mandate it had given him, and declares that some writings do not conform to their doctrine. It claims that if such a judgement is made, it will only be the result of a thorough investigation conducted according to established practice which affords the party concerned the opportunity to clear up possible misunderstandings in this thought.

In all this procedure there seems to be no suggestion that the theologian might be in a position to rectify mistakes and misunderstandings on the part of the *magisterium*. The Instruction somewhere acknowledges that the 'established procedures' might be improved, but it is anxious to make clear that there is no suggestion that this might be a violation of human rights. The Church appears to have a view of 'rights' which differs substantially from that held by secular society. 'To speak in this instance of human rights', says the Instruction, 'is out of place for it indicates a failure to recognise the proper hierarchy of these rights as well as the ecclesial community and her common good.' This departure from the generally accepted norms of academic thought and expression is vigorously defended as the only means available to the *magisterium* to 'defend the right of the people of God to receive the message of the Church in its purity and integrity and not to be disturbed by a particularly dangerous opinion'.

It was not surprising that the publication of the Instruction gave rise to many critical comments, particularly from Roman Catholic academics professionally engaged in teaching and writing theology. There was a widespread feeling that although the Instruction claimed to have been written in a spirit of charity to encourage bishops to maintain and develop good relations of trust with the theologians, it appeared quite deliberately to ferment a spirit of confrontation. The head of one college theological department complained that those who earned their living by teaching theology and had never been involved in public controversy found it insulting to be treated like naughty children. Another said that the model offered in the document for the work of a theologian was not one that would be recognised by anyone teaching in a British state-funded institution.

Those whose faith is based on a fundamental assurance derived either from Scripture as the inerrant Word of God or on the pronouncements of a *magisterium* inspired by the infallible guidance of the Spirit of Christ, have in common a deep concern for an unequivocal proclamation of the gospel of Jesus Christ. God has spoken clearly through his Word or his Church. The trumpet call must not give an uncertain sound. Any teaching which seems to question this assurance is putting the Christian mission at risk. Biblical and ecclesiastical fundamentalism is a well-intentioned exercise in risk avoidance. It holds a strong attraction for many whose single-minded devotion to Christ and his Church is beyond question. They demand in their religious life a no-risk policy. But is it likely that the God who reveals himself in Scripture, in science, and in personal experience as a risk-taking God should expect his Church always to play safe by discouraging the questioning, doubting and exploring spirit that many find leads them into new understanding of truth and fresh experiences of God?

EPISCOPAL DILEMMAS

Somebody once said that the camel is a beast which looks as though it might have been designed by a committee. It is oddly shaped, and slightly comical, yet has proved to be of great use to mankind in its modest way. The Church of England might be allowed a similar description. It is a Church which those who do not belong to it find hard to understand.

It makes great claims that it is firmly founded on Scripture and the ancient traditions of the Christian Church. It is proud to acknowledge the place of reason and conscience in the religious quest. Yet when it seeks the appropriate authority by which to interpret the practical meaning of these great claims, it has to rely on a curious mixture of ingredients from which to derive authoritative guidance. There are forty-three diocesan bishops, men of undoubted integrity but who vary so widely in intelligence, experience and theological knowledge that as soon as they depart from uniting on the most general principles they find themselves disagreeing about almost everything else. There is a General Synod, supported by a proliferation of subsidiary 'experts', which consists of about three hundred men and women, more or less democratically elected, who are probably no wiser nor any more stupid than any reasonable adult body assembled for a serious purpose. There are two long-stops (to use a cricketing term) in the shape of the Prime Minister (who may belong to any church denomination or none) who has a final say in recommending the appointment of bishops and deans, and a secular Parliament, some six hundred MPs and an assortment of Lords who are entitled to give a final judgement on such matters as whether a man who has been divorced and re-married may be ordained to celebrate Holy Communion. Kipling said that a camel's hump is an ugly lump. But the Anglican animal has some advantages as well as disadvantages over other creatures in the ecclesiastical menagerie.

A Church which by choice or historical circumstance finds itself able to take risks with its ambivalent attitude towards authority has its own peculiar contribution to bring to the ecumenical task of proclaiming the Christian gospel to the people it is called to serve. Like many other Christian bodies, it is presently engaged in a serious examination of its authority structures, and asking itself what risks need to be taken and which should be avoided. The examination begins with the bishops. There was a time when bishops were held in high esteem by most people. There was a certain mystique attached to the office. They lived in palaces, were addressed as 'my lord' and their correspondents signed themselves 'your obedient servant'. An episcopal visit to a church was an awesome occasion. Before the coming of the telephone and motor car they were seldom seen by their flocks. Their remoteness was accentuated by their traditional dress of top hat, apron, knee breeches and gaiters. Their appearance differentiated them from the general public and gave them an air of authority. Today, in most walks of life, authority is seldom accepted ex officio. Authority has to be earned. Even when the acceptance of an office grants the right to exercise authority, that authority has to be authenticated by personality, competence, efficiency, and the ability to understand and work with other people. Many bishops today pass this test with flying colours. A few conspicuously fail. The accessibility of bishops to their clergy and people has been of great pastoral advantage, but it can be a threat to their authority. Clergy who at one time invariably addressed their episcopal masters as their lordships, now use their Christian names. Nor are bishops any more immune than other public figures from criticism, caricaturing or debunking in the media.

We have already noted how the Roman Catholic bishops show themselves threatened by the impact of popular democratic ideas on their magisterial authority. They seem to be increasingly self-conscious about their proper place in the hierarchy. Bishops in the Church of England have been showing a similar concern. How do the profound changes taking place in our political, cultural and social life affect the traditional working model of Anglican episcopacy? How can the traditional authoritarianism of a bishop be combined with the democratic processes of synodical government? How can a bishop both 'give a lead' as many demand of him and yet remain obviously and seriously accountable to his diocese? This is an area of ecclesiastical life fraught with risks. The debate centres round the question whether these risks help or hinder the work of the Church in which bishops are called to be leaders and to exercise control.

In 1986 the Archbishops of Canterbury and York set up a working group to consider 'the nature and function of the episcopate'[9] The Cameron Report, named after its chairperson, Chancellor Sheila Cameron QC, was published in the autumn of 1990 and debated in the General Synod in the spring of the following year. It is a weighty document of 300 pages and it is questionable whether the commissioning archbishops expected quite such a bulky work. Much space is devoted to the theology of the episcopate and its historical development. It is particularly concerned to explore the relationship between the bishops and the Holy Trinity which is somewhat obscure. It made one reader wonder whether a similarly divine origin could be accorded by the theologians to the Prime Minister, the Governor of the Bank of England or the Director General of the BBC. The report also follows too easily the temptation of similar ecclesiastical documents to ascribe to the work of the Holy Spirit everything that is happening in the contemporary Church to which the group wishes to give its seal of approval. Yet it is valuable in indicating how a distinguished group of Anglicans understand the problems facing episcopal authority in today's Church of England.

When a bishop is consecrated he is reminded that as chief pastor in his diocese he 'shares with his fellow bishops a special responsibility to maintain and further the unity of the Church, to uphold discipline and guard the faith'. He must publicly affirm his beliefs in 'the doctrine of the Christian faith as the Church of England has received it, and to teach and expound it'. So the Cameron Report affirms that the bishop has a special task of 'safeguarding the continuing fidelity of the Church to the message received and transmitted by the apostles'. But the bishop's teaching office – his primary duty as the focus of unity – bristles with difficulty in the real situation of today. New insights into what is meant by 'the message received from the apostles' are always being discovered in the processes of theological development, biblical scholarship, and the attempts to reformulate doctrines inherited from the long ago past into the language and thought of a very different age. As we saw in a previous chapter, bishops continue to disagree on many aspects of Christian belief even if they sometimes attempt to disguise their disagreement by issuing face-saving reports. A Church which possesses an infallible *magisterium* can avoid this problem, even though profound differences lurk beneath the surface. But the Church of England has no such device, and this is acknowledged honestly in the Cameron Report.

> We must answer that in God's undergirding of our decisions, our human needs and failings are accepted and allowed for, and the mode of our learning together is in tune with the enabling of our growth in holiness through living together in the faith. If God never forces his people's consent it must follow that the Spirit's guidance is not irresistible, and that the Church in history, humanly sinful and fallible, has not necessarily at all points been perfectly responsive to the infallible guide.[10]

The crucial question is whether we can ever dare to say that at any time or at any point the Church has been 'perfectly responsive to the infallible guide of the Spirit'. Because we are humanly sinful and fallible we must be prepared to say that our knowledge of God and his purposes is inevitably partial. It is because of the imperfection of our perception that we are bound to differ from one another in our understanding of matters of emphasis and interpretation of our faith and experience of God. The trial and error of dialectic and 'the correction of one another in Christ' remains an essential element in Christian discipleship. We are not called to submit correct theological answers set by a divine examinations board. We are invited to follow the Living Lord. This is the risk-taking path along which God summons us in our pilgrimage of faith. In the conflicts we face on the journey, the bishop is called to moderate on behalf of his people, providing them with guidance and encouragement when he can. But there is no evidence that a bishop is any more likely to be 'responsive to the infallible guide of the Spirit' than are many of the Christian men and women he is called to serve and lead.

In their report *The Nature of Christian Belief*, the bishops acknowledged this dilemma.

> A bishop may properly enter into questionings on matters of belief, both because as a man of integrity he will feel any force there is in such questioning, and also as a leader part of his responsibility on behalf of the Church is to listen honestly to criticisms of its faith and life. But in all he says he must take care not to present variant beliefs as if they were the faith of the Church; and he must also make as sure as he can that his hearers understand what that faith is and the reason for it.[11]

In the final sentence of that paragraph there is a hint that the bishops were losing their nerve. They knew that there were deep differences on fundamental theological questions among them. They knew that inside most of them there were doubts and fears which they share with many of their clergy and laity. To admit this in public, choosing their words carefully and sensitively, may be of greater encouragement to the more thoughtful members of their flocks than giving the impression that in matters of faith everything is plain sailing for them. An over-simplification of truth proves to be a disservice to the truth itself. A risk-free presentation of the gospel only succeeds in presenting the message in an emasculated form.

The Cameron Report insists that if the bishop is to be an effective teacher of the faith he must take care to listen to his people and be always ready to share their insights. Every member of the Christian community has something to bring to the common good of the Church. Wise bishops will set aside part of their hard-pressed time to meet with men and women from many walks of life, and not necessarily only churchgoers, as much to hear what they have to say to him as to say the things that he has it in mind to tell them. Meeting with the laity in this way may be a more constructive use of their time than involving them in the ever more complex machinery of church bureaucracy. Cameron warns how easily we 'fall into the habit of convening new committees and setting up fresh meetings until those who serve on them find their time and energy disproportionately committed to planning and discussion.'

The development of synodical government in the past twenty years has shifted the balance of authority in the Church of England, and the concept of bishop-in-synod has raised problems which are only just beginning to be faced. The Cameron Report outlines the problem but does not venture a solution, admitting that there are as yet no answers to questions concerning the right balance between episcopal and synodical authority because they have not yet been resolved either in theology or in practice. They have to do not only with the pragmatic allocation of tasks and responsibilities, but also with the theological character of the personal and corporate in episcopal ministry.

CHURCH AND STATE

After twenty years of life the General Synod of the Church of England has embarked on a long process of serious self-examination in the face of increasing criticism and discontent with its manner of working. The Synod has a long history behind it. Before 1919 the Church was governed by the two Convocations of Canterbury and York which met separately, each consisting of a House of Bishops and a House of Clergy. These had their origins way back in the thirteenth century. Early in the present century it came to be recognised that these were very unrepresentative bodies. A 1902 report from the Canterbury Convocation said that 'theology justifies and history demonstrates that the ultimate authority and right of collective action lies with the whole body of the Church and that the co-operation of the clergy and laity in Church government and discipline belongs to the true ideal of the Church.' In 1919 the Church Assembly was formed by Act of Parliament. For half a century it served its purpose as a forum for general discussion by clergy and laity together on Church affairs and for the prep-aration of legislation to be placed before Parliament. But it was an unwieldly body with 750 members (many of them ex-officio) and it was not empowered to make final decisions on matters relating to worship and doctrine. These remained in the hands of the clerical members of the Convocations.

On 11 November 1970 Queen Elizabeth II inaugurated the new General Synod of the Church of England. It consisted of three houses: bishops, clergy and laity. It was half the size of the previous Church Assembly. It was recognised as the supreme legislative body of the Church. Although it did not bring about disestablishment, as some had hoped, it did mark a further step in the diminishing influence of Parliament in Church affairs. Since 1970 it has transacted a huge amount of business, much of it of considerable importance to the Church – and even to the nation. Yet it has drawn to itself an increasing volume of criticism from within its own membership and outside. Clifford Longley of *The Times* went so far as to ask whether it was not now the time for it to die in order to be born again.

God is not a God of blueprints. Nowhere in the Bible is there a carefully worked out plan for Church government. The Holy Spirit has not yet provided a synodical do-it-yourself kit with a clear instruction manual included. The readiness to learn the lessons of past failures and successes, and the courage to explore a new ground, is what the risk-taking God asks of the Church. So a preliminary discussions paper with thirty-eight questions has been widely circulated, covering synodical government at national, diocesan and local levels. When the replies are received and collated, they are expected to provide useful material for a Synodical Government Review Commission.

The nub of the debate will focus on the relationship between autocracy and democracy in a Christian community. Present problems derive from a Church with a long history of autocratic bishops ruling over a comparatively powerless laity. How can such a body take democracy into its system? As a body pretending to democracy, the General Synod has long been considered less than satisfactory. Its membership has been described as elderly, middle-class, right-wing and resistant to change. The poor are not represented. Nor are ethnic minorities. Meetings are usually held at times most suitable for the professional classes, the retired, the leisured and the clergy. Methods of selecting representatives for election to the Synod also come under criticism. There is much pious talk about praying to the Holy Spirit that the 'right' people may be elected. The Holy Spirit receives many nudges from pressure groups who target with their own particular propaganda those entitled to vote. The quasi-Parliamentary stance by which the General Synod operates takes a confrontation model which many see as inappropriate for a Christian assembly. Bishop Hugh Montefiore believes that the fact that the Synod meets in Westminster gives it the illusion of power. 'Can we not think in terms of the family of God working together on different levels for the Kingdom of God?'

It is the weakening of the authority of the bishops which most alarms Canon J. R. Porter, formerly professor of theology in Exeter University and a long-standing Synod member. He asks, 'Is this really the body to make decisions on the great issues of faith and morals by a show of hands? Should not the Synod be based on more explicitly religious models? He argues that historically synods have always been essentially meetings of church leaders – the bishops. The Bishop of Birmingham, Mark Santer, followed this same line of thought in a forthright address to the autumn meeting of his diocesan synod in 1990.

> We often hear calls for strong leadership to be given by the archbishops and bishops. But it is difficult to exercise leadership in a system which is so full of checks and balances as to produce a widely diffused and virtually infinite

power of obstruction on any issue of importance. It must also be admitted that the bishops themselves are so mesmerised by the system that they are hardly ever prepared to make collective use of the powers which they, in fact, possess . . . The synod is the Parliament, who is the government? This is, in fact, a debilitating confusion between the role of government which properly belongs to the episcopate, and the deliberative and legislative role which properly belongs to the synod as a whole. This reveals itself in a confusion and competition as to who is in charge of the Church.

Bishop Santer is not the first bishop to raise a critical voice against the Church of England's machinery of government. Nearly twenty years previously Bishop Mervyn Stockwood wrote in his Southwark diocesan letter that he regards the General Synod as a disaster, 'a playground of bureaucrats and bores wasting time on endless chatter and wasting money on cascades of memoranda and minutes'. More recently Dean John Lang, encountering the General Synod when he moved from his work with the BBC to the deanery of Lichfield, said that it was killing the Church of England: 'The disagreements are endless and their effect is banal.'

It is easier to criticise than to construct. We are here in one of God's risk areas. When the first Christians came to a decision on some important matter of faith or strategy, they were inclined to say that 'it seemed good to the Holy Spirit and to us.' It can be safely presumed that the guidance received did not come to them as a direct message from heaven, but reached them through the influence of a number of channels – personal, emotional, circumstantial, rational, and involving all the normal human factors of temperament, prejudices, fear, hope, power and common sense. Such varied factors play their part in the decision-making not only of the General Synod but of every ecclesial authority and council. This is the price we pay for the freedom God gives us. This is the risk that God is prepared to take whenever Christians meet together in conference. Power struggle in some shape or form is evident in every Christian decision-making body whether it calls itself the *magisterium*, a synod or a prayer meeting. There are no blueprints or working drawings. God takes the astonishing and breathtaking risk of inviting those who belong to the Church to work things out for themselves as best they can. It might have been easier if he had chosen some other way, but those who venture out on the exploration of God's will in faith know that his way is the most rewarding.

In the dying session of the 1990 Parliament Mr Michael Latham presented a private member's bill on the question of Church reform. It had little chance of succeeding, though its proposals were not without interest. He wanted to see the abolition of the General Synod and, in its place, a new Assembly which would have two 'houses', one for all the bishops (diocesan and suffragan) and one for clergy and laity. The Assembly would have power to vote 'on all appropriate matters'. The house of bishops would elect new bishops, subject to final approval by the Crown. The bill would abolish the automatic right of bishops to sit in the House of Lords. Although cries for the disestablishment of the Church of England are heard less frequently than formerly, the question still simmers, as Mr Latham's comparatively modest proposal indicates. From time to time it comes to the boil when Parliament rejects a measure submitted by the Church. The state still remains a partner in the Church of England practice of authority, though it is now less obtrusive than the other two legs of the tripod – the bishops and the Synod who, as we have seen, are engaged in some kind of struggle for power.

The state's stake in ecclesiastical affairs in England has a long history. In the English Reformation the spiritual power of the papacy passed, by Act of Parliament, to the monarch. Henry VIII became the nearest equivalent to the pope. He did not consecrate bishops, but he appointed them. Although he had an interest in theology, he did not define doctrine, but the Convocations could not do their work without his consent. As the political power of the monarchy declined, bishops continued to be appointed by the Crown, but only on the recommendation of the Prime Minister. Measures passed by the Convocations could not receive the Royal Assent until approved by Parliament. In order to fulfil this statutory duty, the monarch had to be in communion with the Church of England.

The Anglican Church is still the Church of the English nation 'by law established' and the English Parliament retains a degree of control over it. In recent years the Church has managed to acquire a considerable degree of liberty without sacrificing its status as the Established Church. Many believe that this provides the Church with a particular opportunity to influence national affairs. They think there is still force in the argument advanced by Frederick Denison Maurice, the nineteenth-century reformer.

> A national Church should mean a Church which exists to purify and elevate the mind of a nation, to give those who minister the laws a sense of the grandeur of the law and the source from whence it proceeds, to tell the rulers of the nations that all false ways are ruinous, that truth is the only stability of our time or any time.

Such a statement might have struck a chord in the hearts of English people a century and a half ago. Does it make any sense in the final decade of the twentieth century? Most English people are religiously neutral. Those who join in Sunday worship attend a number of denominations, with the Established Church in a minority. We have become a multi-racial society with an increasing number of adherents to non-Christian religions. The majority of people probably think of Britain as a secular state. Yet there are many who would say, if asked, that they are glad the Church of England is there. They enjoy its ceremonial involvement on state occasions. They value the parish church, even though they enter it rarely. They value cathedrals as a part of the national heritage and for their contribution to tourism. They value the local vicar, even though they may not know who he is and seldom require his services. Some parents, though a diminishing number, still opt to send their children to Church schools, and men and women in the forces value their chaplains, especially in times of conflict. But it is an open question whether this residue of 'folk religion' helps or hinders the real impact of the gospel, and whether the continuing of an Established Church enhances or weakens the vision of Church and nation which F. D. Maurice described with such optimism.

In 1970 a Commission on Church and State chaired by

Professor Owen Chadwick rejected disestablishment and maintained the prerogative of the Crown to appoint bishops, though half the members wished to exclude the Prime Minister from the procedure. Four years later the General Synod voted overwhelmingly that the Church should have the final say in episcopal appointments. Discussion followed between the Prime Minister (James Callaghan) and the Archbishop of Canterbury (Donald Coggan) who agreed, with the consent of Parliament, to implement the least radical of the Chadwick Commission's proposals. A Crown Appointments Committee of twelve members was set up. Meeting in the strictest confidence, and after the most careful deliberations, it would send two names to the Prime Minister with the expectation that the first would be submitted to the Crown. Recent appointments made under this arrangement, including those of the present Archbishop of Canterbury and Bishop of London, have been accepted as reasonably satisfactory. But is the process democratic enough? In other parts of the Anglican Communion bishops are chosen by the decision of an electoral college of clergy and laity, with their decision ratified by the bench of bishops or some other senior authority. There is strong pressure in the Church of England to follow these more democratic procedures. There is one drawback. Democratic procedures have a tendency to choose 'safe' candidates who are likely to be most acceptable to the majority. This can result in a monochrome bench of bishops. In a system where the leadership exercises a corporate responsibility it is essential to provide a collegiality of varied talents and experience ranging from the most conservative to the most radical. It takes all sorts to make a Church, and this should be reflected in the leadership. Democratic systems may avoid risk at the price of dull mediocrity. A leadership which pleases everybody will end up in creating a static Church. This is a strong reason for retaining the present system (or something like it) in the Church of England. It is an open question whether the Holy Spirit (presuming that he has anything to do with ecclesiastical appointments) finds it easier to work through the occupant of the chair of St Peter with his theological prejudices, or through a committee of twenty United Reformed Church members who might be a rather cumbersome talking shop, or through a Prime Minister, who may be under political pressure,

selecting one of the names submitted to him by the Appointments Committee, or simply, as the apostles did, saying some
prayers and then tossing up for it. Each method has its obvious
drawbacks. None can claim to provide the perfect way of
appointing people who are claimed by some Churches to be the
successors to the apostles. Perhaps God intends the Churches
to take one another's experiences seriously so that they may
work together towards a better solution.

A comparatively minor revision of the 1662 Book of Common
Prayer, including changes which were already illegally in use,
was overwhelmingly accepted by the Church Assembly in 1927.
When the measure to legalise its use was presented to Parliament it was twice rejected, largely due to pressure from a
group of evangelical MPs (not all of them Anglican) who were
suspicious of 'Romanising tendencies'. The defeat in Parliament
of an ecclesiastical measure for which the Church had shown
great enthusiasm, raised a new clamour for disestablishment.
Eventually a compromise device was adopted by the bishops,
who made it known that they had a legal right to authorise
special liturgical forms for use in their own dioceses. By this
means, the 1928 Prayer Book came into common use though it
was soon recognised to be far from satisfactory. In the light of
this half-hearted experiment the Church of England was able
to produce a legally authorised Alternative Services Book fifty
years later. This may seem an odd way of setting about God's
business, but it provides an interesting corroboration of faith in
a God whose activities in creation proceed by means of trial
and error – a risky process which ultimately can lead to satisfactory results.

The 1928 Prayer Book fiasco and its eventual outcome did
not close the disestablishment debate. It rumbled on for many
years, though most people no longer consider it a major priority
in the face of so many more pressing issues on the ecclesiastical
agenda. But in 1990 the question was reopened in a curious
way. In July of that year the General Synod sent the Clergy
Ordination Measure to the House of Commons. This would
allow the Archbishops of Canterbury and York to permit the
ordination of someone who had divorced and remarried whilst
the first spouse was still living. The measure was approved by
the House of Lords but rejected in the House of Commons by

a narrow majority. The General Synod, not ready to take No for an answer, sent the measure back. This time it was approved by 228 votes to 106 after a lively and well-attended debate. Some members gave voice to the peculiar situation in which the Church of England seemed here to be at odds both with Parliament and with its own convictions about the sanctity of marriage. Archbishop Runcie had to explain that this did not lift the general ban against the ordination of divorced and remarried people; it would merely allow occasional exception to the Church's rule! This incident seemed to suggest a reversal of what might have been expected. Parliament was concerned about the morals of the nation: the Church was concerned about its own freedom to act. There followed a spate of articles and correspondence in the press, evenly divided between those in favour and those opposed to the disestablishment of the Church of England. Those in favour of the status quo believed that the procedures necessary for disestablishment would occupy the attention of the Church for many years when it had more important things to do. It would indicate a failure of nerve and add to the feeling of rootlessness which is widely felt in all levels of society. It would weaken the position of the monarch and deprive the nation of the grace and dignity which the Church has been able to bring to public occasions. If the concept of a 'national church' were to be lost, the bishops would lose their seats in the House of Lords, the parochial clergy would lose their special position in their own local society, and the Church would lose many opportunities for serving the nation in the many ways that establishment allows.

Critics of the present situation believe that these arguments are no longer valid. They over-exaggerate the influence of the Church of England and underestimate the growing importance of other Churches. In the present ecumenical climate it has to be questioned whether it is appropriate to retain the concept of a state religion as conferring special privilege and status on one denomination out of many others also trying to exercise a Christian ministry in a pluralist society. They also believe that Christian influence in society is not primarily effected by the presence of bishops in the House of Lords but by the Christian understanding of lay men and women as they go about the business of their daily lives.

The debate continues with the pros and cons fairly evenly balanced. Adrian Hastings, the Roman Catholic theologian and historian, who might be considered a dispassionate observer of Anglican affairs, writes about the prospect of disestablishment:

> Christianity and English society would be further weakened without any real compensatory advantages. If what little remains of the church establishment were cut in principle away the Church of England would be repudiating too much of its past history, and that is never wise to do, especially in a time of admitted weakness.[12]

But David Jenkins, the Bishop of Durham, who preceded Adrian Hastings in the chair of theology in the University of Leeds, takes a robust view to the contrary. He describes the legal link between the state and the Church in England as 'a vestigial rigmarole left over from the Middle Ages – a kind of Gilbert and Sullivan performance which on occasions goes down well on television'. It must go, he insists, because it speaks of past history rather than present realities. From the Christian point of view being an Established Church must increasingly and seriously obscure what the gospel of Jesus Christ is all about.

It is safe to predict that the present arrangement will change sooner or later. Whether it is wise to cling to the status quo for as long as possible or to force change as quickly and cleanly as possible or to let things take their course without either holding back or forcing the pace – these options in both Church and state will continue to divide opinion. Whatever steps are eventually taken (or not taken), risk will be involved. Once again we find that there are no easy solutions. That is the way of the Church – and always will be.

This chapter has been a discussion on the various ways in which Churches of different traditions have attempted to find the source for authoritative guidance in matters of belief and Church organisation. They have come to very different conclusions. Fundamentalists claim to see in the literal acceptance of Scripture as the Word of God absolutely clear guidance. Roman Catholics believe that it is the will of God for his Church that authority has been given to those who have been granted in an infallible *magisterium* the insights into the correct interpretation of Scripture and tradition. Anglicans, concerned to find the right interaction between discipline and freedom, search for a compromise between the given authority of Scripture and tradition on the one side and the individual right due to reason and conscience on the other. Each approach carries its own advantages and disadvantages. The authoritarian stance of biblical and ecclesiastical fundamentalism has great attraction, particularly in times of uncertainty when people demand a clear lead from their religion. But biblical fundamentalism is challenged by critical scholarship and ecclesiastical dogmatism can only be acceptable at the cost of sacrificing the freedom of rational and conscientious enquiry. The Anglican attempt to combine authority with democracy together with the inheritance of an established religion often appears in public as fudged, confused and at sixes and sevens with itself. Each approach has its own risks. Not only are we all subject to the fallibility of human judgement, but the Bible gives us no clear guidance on any of the matters discussed in this chapter. If the New Testament had provided us with a clear blueprint on how the Church should order the details of its community life and faith, there would presumably be general agreement about these things among Christians of all persuasions. Because we have been denied clear instructions, we can only presume that this is how God intends it to be. This is part of the divine trial and error syndrome. Because God has taken the risk of allowing the Christian family to explore different paths towards the same goal, so each separate tradition has to challenge its own understanding in the light of the answers their fellow Christians have given. If this diversity makes life more awkward for us all, this is precisely what the risk-taking God demands of us. Playing safe has no part in true discipleship.

6

MINISTRY

NECESSARY CHANGE

BISHOP LESSLIE NEWBIGIN once remarked that although different Christian traditions follow different orders and concepts of ministry, they all claim that what they practice has firm foundations in Scripture. He said that it reminded him of the caucus race in *Alice in Wonderland*. Everybody wins; everybody has prizes. The risk-taking God appears to have taken one of his greatest risks in the history of the Church of Jesus Christ.

The preface to the ordination service in the 1662 Book of Common Prayer states with great conviction that 'It is evident unto all men diligently reading Holy Scripture and ancient authors that from the Apostles' time there have been three orders of ministers in Christ's Church; Bishops, Priests and Deacons.' Most students reading Holy Scripture would not find it so evident. In the earliest days there seems to have been an assortment of recognised ministries entrusted with the task of 'equipping God's people for their work in his service'. It was not long before the three-fold form of ministry developed into the way that the majority of Churches understand it today. In consequence a further dividing line came to be drawn between those in holy orders and various lay ministries. Yet there have always been questions about the status and job description of those in holy orders and their relationship with the lay ministers who sometimes appear to be fulfilling equally essential tasks in the life and ministry of the Church.

It can be convincingly argued that there is no absolute proof in Scripture that the type of ministry which eventually emerged from the New Testament was divinely intended to be handed down from generation to generation without question or change. The Church itself has always been subject to change made necessary by new theological insights, new ecclesiological needs and new ways of understanding human relationships. The Roman Catholic theologican Edward Schillebeeckx once said that 'the constant in the Church's ministry is to be found only in specific historically changing forms'. The God who once upon a time revealed himself in the Incarnate Lord, continues to make himself known through the process of history. The Church is part of that historical process. It is logical to assume that he has provided the Church with a pattern of ministry flexible enough to respond to the ever changing circumstances of succeeding centuries. The Bible does not provide an ecclesiastical blueprint valid for ministry for all time. It plants seeds which grow if carefully nurtured.

The character of ministry has changed throughout the centuries. It is certain that many more changes lie ahead. Some are already taking place. The Lima Statement on Faith and Order of the World Council of Churches declared that traditional patterns of ministry must not be allowed to inhibit the growth of new ministerial patterns.

> The community which lives in the power of the Spirit will be characterized by a variety of charisms. The Spirit is the giver of diverse gifts which enrich the life of the community. In order to enhance their effectiveness the community will recognise publicly certain of these charisms. While some serve permanent needs in the life of the community, others will be temporary. Men and women in the communities of religious orders fulfil a service which is of particular importance for the life of the Church. The ordained ministry, which is itself a charism, must not become a hindrance for the variety of these charisms. On the contrary, it will help the community to discover the gifts bestowed on it by the Holy Spirit and will equip members of the body to serve in a variety of ways.[1]

This chapter does not intend to offer a thorough dissertation on the present crisis in ministry, nor to explore the potential for a great expansion in modes of ministry which the Lima statement envisaged. Here the purpose is more modest. It is to look at those areas of ministry which are particularly under scrutiny in the British Churches, and to discuss what risks need to be taken now in order to fulfil their ministry to society in the coming decades. In the Church of England the shortage of clergy is already being met by non-stipendiary ministers, locally based ministries and the increasing responsibility afforded to the laity. The ordination of women to the priesthood and ultimately to the episcopate, is on the agenda. From the Roman Catholic experience questions arise about the traditional image of the priesthood, what changes are needed to meet the contemporary situation, and to ask whether the continuation of compulsory celibacy is a help or a hindrance to the Catholic priest at work in a modern parish. Honest answers to these questions involve the possibility of taking necessary risks.

When it became obvious that the number of candidates offering themselves for ordination in the Church of England was falling far short of requirements and that a sharp decline in the number of priests was imminent, the central authorities printed a little slogan which was to be displayed on parish notice boards. It simply said, 'Pray more for your clergy: Pray for more clergy.' The first part of the slogan was unexceptionable. The second raised awkward questions. Was it encouraging us to tell God that he was making a great mistake in not supplying his Church with enough clergy, and would he please do something about it as soon as possible? Perhaps the shortfall in the number of priests was God's way of pointing out to a reluctant Church that there was a good supply of women waiting to be ordained who would prove to be equally as qualified and effective as men for the job. Perhaps he was also saying that in the Church there were huge resources of lay men and women waiting to be used in many aspects of ministry, and that until they were taken seriously in the ministry of the priesthood of all believers, the Church did not deserve to have any more clergy.

Far from being a calamity, the shortage of clergy should be seen as a divine hint that the whole business of professional ministry needs to be given close scrutiny. If the ecclesiastical car is to be allowed to stay on the road, it needs a drastic MOT test, followed by a big repair job – including, perhaps, a new engine. The source of man- and woman-power for the effective deployment of ministry is controlled not only by past tradition (which may be paralysing) but also by the realities of present experience. Many young men and women look at the Church today and come to the conclusion that there are better opportunities elsewhere for their idealism and their desire to be of service. The secularisation of society raises difficult questions about the role of the full-time clergy and the viability ôf the parochial system which has been the basis of ecclesiastical life in England for a thousand years. The steady decline in the number of entrants into the ministry of the Church of England in the past thirty years is unlikely to show much change for the better in the forseeable future. A sudden and unexpected increase on a large scale might solve some problems and be a sign of divine intervention. But the availability of more clergy of the traditional kind might give the Church the excuse to by-pass the more radical thinking about ministry to which God seems to be calling synods and congregations today. The continuation of clerical manpower shortage might be of positive good for the Church until the basic problems of ministry have been courageously faced and new solutions put into action.

Staffing levels raise serious difficulties in urban areas, particularly in inner cities and on large housing estates. In the country it is now common to find a single parish priest in charge of six or more villages, each with its fine parish church and the expectation of some sort of parochial independence. In some areas help is available from retired clergy and licensed Readers. But this is not an adequate solution. The Archbishops' Commission on Rural Areas (1990) viewed the situation with a mixture of hope and alarm.

> Our deliberations have convinced us that the decline in clergy numbers in rural areas is opening the way to a new and cohesive vision of the Church's ministry. We believe this to be the work of the Holy Spirit. This has not, however, been achieved without profound and, in some cases, harrowing effect.[2]

Among responses to this crisis the likelihood of ordination of women to the priesthood offers one important solution. More men are being made priests while retaining their secular employment. There are some important experiments in the creation of a strictly local priesthood of non-stipendiary clergy. There is a far distant prospect (which would be strongly contested) that certain respected lay men and women might be authorised to preside at Holy Communion as some are now allowed to administer the sacrament. Each of these suggestions involves greater or lesser risk to traditional concepts of ministry. Yet the *status quo* offers no likelihood of an ultimate solution for the future well-being of the Church. To remain where we always have been may be far more damaging than daring to take the plunge of radical and controversial solutions.

For a long time there have been priests exercising their ministry outside the parochial system, and paid by secular authorities. They include university professors, BBC religious programme producers, chaplains in the prison service, hospitals and schools. Their ministry is accepted as a genuine priestly ministry, though their fellow clergy are sometimes a little envious that these colleagues are able to earn larger salaries than are available to ordinary parish priests. But in recent years there has come into being a new brand of priests. These are those who in secular employment feel a call to holy orders but wish to continue their secular work for which they have been trained and by which they will continue to earn their living. They have increased rapidly in numbers, and are able to give valuable assistance in the parochial ministry. But they raise a number of questions which have to be answered. Are ordained ministers in secular employment to be considered as 'part-time ministers' or even 'not proper clergy'? The official answer to that question is a firm No. There is only one priesthood. There can be no distinctions between amateurs and professionals. There are no 'pass degree priests' and 'honours degree priests'. If you are a priest you are a priest – always and everywhere. It is for this reason that the Church of England has insisted that all candidates for the ministry, whether stipendiary or non-stipendiary, should have their suitability assessed by exactly the same criteria. There must be no temptation to provide a convenient short-cut to ordination in view of the shortage of clergy to fill the vacant posts, or the shortage of money to pay them.

But there are some who question the wisdom of this rigorous policy. In July 1988 Archbishop Keith Rayner came from Australia to give his reflection at a London conference for ministers in secular employment. He said:

> It seems to me that there is a need for an authorised ordained ministry in secular employment who do not have, and never will have, and should not have, the kind of qualifications which we traditionally require for a priest in the Church of England. One thing that has struck me this weekend – and this is no reflection on you – is how middle class you are. In our present way of working we are making virtually no impact on the great mass of people whom we call 'working class', who are the very ones the Anglican Church throughout the world fails to reach.[3]

The majority of those who are ordained and continue in secular employment are people such as teachers, civil servants, architects, social workers, engineers, pharmacists, and those who are in middle management or self-employed. It is excellent that such people should bring their varied secular experiences into the ministry. But Archbishop Rayner's point needs to be taken.

There are other questions which also need to be tackled. What do those who enter the ministry in this way bring to the Church and what, if anything, do they take to their secular employment? To the Church they can bring much-needed companionship and partnership to single-handed vicars who can easily feel 'out on their own' in their jobs. Earning his living in a secular occupation, as most of his congregation does, should enable the non-stipendiary priest to help his hearers to link their faith and prayers with the daily life of the workplace. He can help them to see that Christianity is not a leisure-time activity, and that God is as much active in industry, commerce, education, social welfare, politics and the ordinary stuff of life as he is in the Church. But what can he bring as a priest to the place where he works and the people who work with him? This is a much more difficult question.

Ministers in secular employment are not worker priests after the French pattern. They do not go to their place of work in order to convert or proselytise. They are not industrial chaplains in disguise. They go to work, like all their fellow employees, to earn a living. If an ordained priest in this kind of ministry was thought to be some kind of Christian secret agent, the management would rightly have their suspicions aroused. An ordained man (or woman) like any other Christian, will do his best to be a good worker and an acceptable colleague; but if he consciously made it known that he was being a good worker 'for the sake of Jesus Christ' most of his colleagues in the workplace would come to think of him as an intolerable prig. Peter Baelz, former Dean of Durham has written:

> The secular world in which the ordained minister is employed is and remains secular and his ordination does not, as such, equip him with some secular skill or competence, whether as a teacher, counsellor, or something similar. In his secular work secular conditions prevail. If, for example, he is a good teacher, that is because he has learned the skills of teaching, not because of any grace of orders. If, on the other hand, he is a bad teacher, the fact that he is ordained provides him with no excuse. His ordination is a sign and reminder that the secular is never self-sufficient, since it has its origin, ground and fulfilment in the kingdom of God',[4]

This is wise advice. Yet it is the experience of some ministers in secular employment that as it becomes known in the workplace that they are 'in the Church' some of their fellow employees may expect them to exercise some form of pastoral ministry. One priest spoke of himself as becoming a sort of informal ecclesiastical information bureau for some of his colleagues. As the only priest some of them may have ever met at close quarters, he was found useful to answer questions about the baby's baptism, or daughter's wedding or how to cope with a funeral and the bereavement which came with it. There is no harm in this, provided that the priest-worker always remembers that his first loyalty is to his employer who pays his wages to do his job, and not to act as an unofficial chaplain.

There are many positive advantages to the Church as the work of priests in secular employment develops. Yet some people feel strongly that this secularisation of the clergy is putting the whole traditional concept of priesthood in jeopardy. Is not the priest called to be 'a man apart'? This was certainly the intention of the ordination service in the Book of Common Prayer, where the ordained is exhorted:

> Seeing that you cannot by any other means compass the doing of so weighty a work pertaining to the salvation of man, but with doctrine and exhortation taken out of the Holy Scriptures, and with a life agreeable to the same; consider how studious ye ought to be in reading and learning the Scriptures, and in framing the manners both of yourselves, and of them that specially pertain unto you, according to the rule of the same Scriptures: and for this self-same cause, how ye ought to foresake and set aside (as much as you may) all worldly cares and studies.

Later in the ordination service the same point is driven home forcibly when the bishop puts a question to each ordinand demanding that they will 'lay aside the study of the world and the flesh' in order to be 'diligent in prayers, and in reading of the Holy Scriptures and in such studies as help to the knowledge of the same'. This instruction to follow the path of 'otherworldliness' goes against the grain of much modern theological and pastoral study. Yet there are those who believe that this is a vital concept of the character of a priest which is in danger of being lost. Does not the authority of the priest demand a certain style of holiness which should distance him from the normal secular life around him? Does not his clerical dress mark him out as a man apart? Is not sufficient time for prayer and biblical study an absolute priority for him if he is to be fully equipped spiritually and mentally for his task? Should he not be 'on call' day and night to be available at a moment's notice to meet urgent pastoral situations? Is a recorded voice on the answerphone an adequate substitute? Can a full working day in the office, town hall department, shop, surgery or schoolroom provide the space needed to fulfil what is generally considered to be the traditional role of the parish priest?

These questions are not easy to answer. There is no doubt that the ministers in full-time secular employment help to relieve the great need in the present shortage of full-time priests. They can also bring a new dimension to an understanding of the nature of priesthood that the authors of the Book of Common

Prayer could not envisage. On the other hand, if priests in secular employment were to become the majority, and this is not beyond the bounds of possibility, will some aspects of priesthood long cherished in the Church of England be lost for ever – to the great detriment of the total ministry of the Church? There is no doubt that great changes lie ahead both in the theology and practice of ministry. The clock cannot, and must not, be put back. But it has to be recognised that equal risks are involved in clinging doggedly to tradition and moving headlong into what is innovative. The future health of the Church lies not only in readiness to change, but in the ability to make careful evaluation of changes as they occur.

MINISTRY AT THE GRASS ROOTS

The chapter headings in the book in which Karl Rahner discussed the future shape of the Church make very clear what shape he hoped would evolve. He looked forward to a 'Declericalised Church', a 'Church from the Roots' and a 'Democratised Church'. Alongside the established parish system, and perhaps eventually replacing it, he hoped to see a Church built up from what he called 'basic communities'. The Church would no longer exist through the mere persistence of the clerical organisation which keeps it going, the public opinion that expects it to be there or the system of recruitment by which children are baptised and indoctrinated by the Church and, to some extent copy the lifestyle of their parents. Rahner said that the Church would only continue to exist by being constantly renewed by a free decision of faith and the formation of congregations on the part of individuals in the midst of a secular society which bears no imprint of Christianity. Instead of the old parish system, he saw a new Church rising up out of the decline of the old, no longer organised 'from above' but through basic Christian communities which have been built up from below.

> When living Christian communities are formed by the Christians themselves, when they possess and attain a certain structure, solidity and permanence, they have just as much right as a territorial parish to be recognised as a basic

element of the Church, as a Church of the bishop's Church
and of the whole Church, even though their concrete basis
of association is not a territory marked out by diocesan
authorities.[5]

How could such a basic community avoid breaking away altogether from the institutional Church and becoming a form of
congregationalism? Rahner answers that when such a community comes into existence from below, formed through the
free decision of faith of its members, it has the right to be
recognised as Church by the episcopal great Church, and to
have its community leader similarly recognised through ordination as long as he can fulfil the necessary functions.

> It is quite compatible with the nature of the hierarchically
> constituted Catholic Church as a whole for such a basic
> community to present to the bishop a suitable leader
> coming from their midst and expect for the latter a relative
> ordination and recognition for this particular community
> as a legal right. The qualities and conditions required for
> such a full community leader (also as leader of the Euchar-
> ist) cannot be decided in the light of who could carry out
> his duties elsewhere . . . They must be seen as related to
> this basic community and the requirements of its leadership
> in the concrete situation. We can set aside without hesi-
> tation the express or tacit assumption that someone can be
> a leader in a Christian community appointed in virtue of
> his ordination (a 'priestly leader') only if he can exercise
> this function successfully, at least in principle, anywhere at
> all without regard to the particular community.[6]

When Rahner goes on to consider the kind of people who
might be suitable for priestly ordination within this basic local
community leadership, he is of the opinion that the obligation
of celibacy must not be imposed, and that a woman as much as
a man could be suitable for this localised priesthood.

When Rahner put these ideas to the Roman Catholic bishops
in Germany nearly a quarter of a century ago, they must have
seemed very revolutionary. Even today the possibility of independent para-parochial groups such as he suggested does not

hold much favour with Roman Catholics or Anglicans in Great Britain. They seem to be taking too many risks. Yet in many parts of the world where the mission of the Church is gravely frustrated by a severe shortage of priests, the possibility of providing an adequate ministry for locally based eucharistic communities is firmly on the agenda.

Already in the Church of England the concept of a locally ordained ministry, selected, approved and supported by the local congregation, is under discussion and in some areas is beginning to be put into practice. Although a departure from the long-established parochial ministry with all the risks that any change inevitably involves, this may be pointing the way to the most significant development in the life of the English Church for many centuries. Strong encouragement for projects designed to create local ordained ministries in Urban Priority Areas was given by the Archbishop of Canterbury's Commission's report *Faith in the City*. It gave three reasons why such a ministry was essential for the furtherance of the Church's work in the inner cities. It creates a fully local Church, deriving its identity from the people in a particular place, working out the way of living faithfully to the gospel by taking full account of the local culture. It reconciles the local Church to the local community, encouraging a close identity between the two. It can be seen as part of the recognition by the Church that traditional ways alone will not enable it to meet its responsibility to local Christian communities in such areas.[7] It is notable that *Faith in the City* is not primarily concerned with the problem of staffing in its strong advocacy of a local ordained ministry. It sees it as a means of rediscovering the Church as genuinely looking outwards towards the local community and participating fully in it. 'To convert the Church to the importance of recognising the leadership of some local people by ordination could therefore be regarded as an important sign of the Church's commitment to promoting a truly local Church at the heart of the wider Church.'

The need for a drastic overhaul of traditional patterns of ministry is even more obvious in rural areas. Single-handed vicars have charge of six or more small scattered villages, maintaining a rather haphazard ministry with the help of peripatetic Readers and retired clergy. Congregations often consist on average of fifteen or twenty people – sometimes less – the majority of them of pensionable age. These loyal congregations deserve the highest praise. Without them their local church would have closed many years ago. They support their services and maintain their lovely church buildings with loyalty and devotion. But the times of worship are of necessity erratic, the quality of the ministry they receive from such a medley of visitors is haphazard. Those who support their local church in rural areas tend to be conservative and resistant to change, suspicious of new liturgical forms or unfamiliar patterns of parochial strategy. But the present situation is unsatisfactory, the outlook uncertain. The more they sense that the future of their own parish church is in jeopardy, the more they wish to cling to the old familiar ways. But the failure to accept change is likely to lead to even greater risk, putting the future of their village churches in greater peril.

Yet there are many churches in small rural communities which are splendid exceptions to this general picture. This may be partly due to an incumbent who sets about this difficult task with imagination and enthusiasm. It often depends even more on lay men and women who have been enabled and encouraged to exercise their own particular ministry within their community. This is why some village churches appear to flourish when there is a vacancy at the vicarage. The laity discover that the well-being of their local church depends entirely on them. It is sad to note that sometimes with the appointment of a new incumbent the men and women who have exercised such a creative role during the interregnum feel that they should now take a back seat.

It is in some rural dioceses in England where the most interesting experiments in local ordained non-stipendiary ministry are taking place. Lincoln diocese began working seriously on this problem as long ago as 1979 and has now established a considerable network of local ordained ministry in the villages of the Lincolnshire countryside. The brief description which follows is largely based on the Lincoln experience. Basic to this conception of local ordained ministry is the creation of a collaborative team of ordained and lay ministers who are chosen locally and selected by the whole congregation. In times of increased bureaucracy in the Church, this is a serious attempt to encourage the local church to manage its own affairs with a renewed sense of responsibility for ministry and mission. Before a local ministry team can be established in a parish or cluster of parishes, a careful audit must be undertaken and sent to the bishop. If he considers it prudent to proceed, the parochial church council will send him the names of those men and women they would recommend as forming their ministerial group. If, after appropriate investigation, the bishop accepts these names, they will undergo a three-year training course organised by the diocese in collaboration with the parish. From the start the congregation commits itself to this collaborative style of ministry.

The members of the ministry team are selected and trained to perform specific tasks in the parish such as pastoral care, liturgical leadership, educational work, administration and other tasks which have traditionally been the sole responsibility of a jack-of-all-trades vicar. From within this ministry team one member is likely to be nominated for priestly office, if he (or she) is called to this particular ministry. Normally the priest's vocation has been thought to derive both from the inner promptings of the Spirit, and from the outward call of the Church. In local ministry it is his own congregation which nurtures his vocation and is the outward instrument of his calling. The candidate for priesthood needs to submit to the rigorous selection procedure provided by the central organisation of the Church or by his local diocesan bishop. He needs to be judged as suitable to work in a ministry shared with a lay team of which he remains an integral member. He also has to work under the direction of a local incumbent who is likely to have oversight of a cluster of villages and a number of local ministry teams. It is probable that this area vicar had some part in fostering his vocation to local priestly ministry. A problem may arise for him when his area vicar has to move to another parish and he must remain in the same place where he earns his living by his secular work. Developing satisfactory relationships may demand much of his gifts of sensitivity and humility.

This local non-stipendiary ministry is still in its infancy. It remains a risky adventure. It raises many difficult problems. Perhaps the most difficult arises from the paradox that the local non-stipendiary priest is ordained into the life-long priesthood of the Universal Church, yet is permitted by the terms of his licence to exercise his priestly ministry only in a carefully defined local area. His licence is likely to be limited initially for a specific period, probably for three years, renewable from time to time. He will also be given a precise job description which is carefully reviewed with him every time his licence is renewed or when there is a change of incumbent. He must also undergo a regular job-appraisal with an authorised adviser. These strict regulations indicate that the local non-stipendiary ministry is still in a vulnerable experimental stage, and for the sake of the Church and of the individuals concerned, careful monitoring is essential. There are many pitfalls to be avoided, many risks to be taken. What happens if his secular work by which he earns his living necessitates a move to a different part of the country? He will not automatically be able to exercise his priesthood in the new parish where he will worship. Already this situation has arisen, creating uncomfortable difficulties. If the scheme persists, such difficulties are unavoidable. But if adequate eucharistic provision is to be available on a regular basis as the focal point of the corporate life of every Christian congregation, the only alternative to the ordination of a local indigenous priesthood would be for certain lay men (and women) to be duly authorised and commissioned to preside at the Holy Communion in their own parishes. This might be a preferable alternative. It would solve some problems, but would create many more. There are risks either way.

Chaos is rightly feared. But in consenting to experimentation in new patterns of ministry to meet new needs, the Church must avoid the error common to many organisations and institutions, of offering new freedoms to its members with one hand, and taking them away with the other. In ministry, as in other facets of Church life, readiness to take risks is an essential ingredient of progress. Timid bishops and cowardly synods must remember that they themselves are part of the evidence that God takes great risks with his Church.

WOMEN IN MINISTRY

That women should be admitted to the priesthood seems to many Christians the most obvious idea in the world. To others it is an evil risk which the Church must not take unless it wants to betray the past. In recent years the debate within the Anglican communion has been seen either as a mild storm in a teacup, or as a deadly brew in a witches' cauldron. It has involved hours of bitter discussion in synods and mountains of minutes, reports and letters to the press. The debate is slowly moving to a final decision. But there is no clear consensus in the Church of England whether guidance one way or another has been given from on High, or whether (as seems probable) no divine guidance is available and we have been left to use our common sense, come to our own conclusions, and live with the consequences. God often appears to prefer that way of working, as if, like the rest of us, he hopes that it will come out right in the end. Whatever the final outcome, the risk element will remain for a long time.

The reasons for and against the ordination of women to the priesthood have been rehearsed so often that there is little need to repeat them here except in bare outline. As in many other ecclesiastical controversies in the Church of England, extremes on the two wings, evangelical and anglo-catholic, unite to oppose schemes which seem to them to contradict traditional forms and practices as they understand them. It is a curious alliance between two factions who base their opposition on quite different propositions. For the evangelicals, Scripture is clear that 'man is the head of the woman'. Both the creation story in Genesis and the writings of St Paul testify to the concept of male leadership and female submission. 'God gave authority to man over woman,' writes one leading evangelical. 'This is part of the pattern set by God. It is not for us to change it or play about with it.' The logic of this is that a woman may preach if she believes that God has called her to do so (in spite of St Paul's apparent prohibition of women teaching) but she must not preside at the Eucharist. That is a male prerogative as a leader in the congregation. The anglo-catholic position is different. The gospel does not demand the subordination of women to men. They have complementary roles. When the priest celebrates the sacrament and announces 'This is my Body' and 'This is my Blood', he is acting as a living icon of Christ. To have a woman in that role would be to give a false image proclaiming a false message. This has been the firm tradition from the beginning and our task, in the words of Bishop Graham Leonard, is 'to stand for the unchanging gospel and to proclaim it without compromise in the situation in which God has called us to do so, no matter what the cost'.

There are others who would not want to label themselves either anglo-catholic or evangelical who question whether one section of the world-wide Church has the right to change a sacred tradition handed down from the past. What right, they ask, has the Church of England to make a unilateral decision on so vital a matter simply because of changing ideas about the place of women in secular society? The ecumenical argument has some strength. The vast majority of Christians are served only by a male priesthood. For the Church of England to depart from this almost universal practice would jeopardise even further any hope of unity with Rome, and make unity with Orthodoxy even more remote. Our Lord's promise that the Holy Spirit would lead his people into all truth was made to the whole Church, not to selected individuals or communities within it. No one group, it is argued, has the right to go it alone.

Those who support the ordination of women fail to be convinced by any of these arguments. They insist that a case cannot be made simply by quoting isolated texts out of context. Most New Testament scholars believe that St Paul's much-quoted statement about man being the 'head of woman' was to do with marriage in the context of the social conventions of his own day, and has nothing to do with the ordination of women. Nor does the icon argument convince them. The priest stands at the altar to represent Christ to the people not in his maleness but in his humanity. The appeal to tradition ignores that fact that the Church in its teaching and practice has often changed course during its history, beginning with the risky decision in its earliest years not to insist that Gentiles should subscribe to the tenets and customs of Judaism before being accepted as Christians. Supporters of women's ordination have been at pains to show that their decision is not made under the influence of contemporary feminism, but is based on Scripture and Christian conscience. The Creator has made both male and female in his image, thus according to both sexes equal dignity. In the New Testament story women have a role unusual in the culture of those times, from the Virgin Mary to the women who were witnesses of the resurrection, and those who appear from time to time in dominant roles in the story of the first Christian communities in the Acts of the Apostles and the Epistles. Paul speaks of the Christian community as the place where there is neither male nor female. So they ask, why does the Church continue to treat women as second class members?

Although opposition to the ordination of women is generally associated with the two 'wings' of the Church of England, there are many who think of themselves as loyal evangelicals or anglo-catholics who refuse to take the acceptable party line. Canon Michael Saward of St Paul's Cathedral, a prominent evangelical, wrote to *The Times*:

> I shall vote for those procedures leading towards the ordination of women because I believe that the New Testament offers a new status to women in the divine covenant; because I also believe that some developments which are consistent with Scripture (e.g. the abolition of slavery) often take centuries before they emerge into Christian consciousness; I further believe that human reason (a subordinate authority) is coming to grasp the conviction that the ordination of women is no longer inappropriate.

From the other end of the ecclesiastical spectrum, a letter came to the *Church Times* from eleven bishops claiming to have been nourished in the Catholic tradition of the Church of England who, on the ground that the unity of Christ is best forwarded when every Christian is true to their own vision of the gospel, wished to make public their own conviction: 'Anglican catholics who support the ordination of women are loyal to the tradition in which our spirituality has grown, and justified in the belief that such ordination can be a precious gift from God to enhance the catholicity of the Church and enrich her mission.' That letter stirred up plenty of mud in the columns of the Church press. The principal of a well-known theological college described the bishops (in the cricketing language enjoyed by ecclesiastics) as 'a third eleven'. Another correspondent, with an absence of charity which sometimes characterises religious controversy, wrote: 'To their Lordships – All I can say is that your hands are the hands of Esau, but your voice is the voice of Jacob, and, like Esau, you are bent on distortion and contempt.'

Outside the Church of England the Free Churches – Methodist, Baptist and United Reformed Churches – employ women ministers with increasing acceptability and decreasing prejudice. The Church of Scotland, which also ordains women, recently reported a welcome change of attitude but confessed that there was still a long way to go. The same judgement can describe those parts of the Anglican communion where the risk of ordaining women as priests, and in two instances as bishops, has been taken. After initial problems it is generally agreed that the Church has been enriched by female ministry. Once the step has been taken most people wonder what all the fuss was about.

The ordination of women to the priesthood raises more difficult problems in the relations between the Anglican Church and the Church of Rome. Pope John Paul II made it clear to Archbishop Runcie that if the Church of England ordained women the prospect of growing unity between the two Churches would be placed in some jeopardy. In 1976 the Roman Catholic Sacred Congregation for the Doctrine of the Faith examined the question at the request of the Pope. It firmly stated that it was necessary to recall that 'the Church, in fidelity to the example of our Lord does not consider herself authorised to admit women to priestly ordination.' This would seem to close the door, if it were not for the well-known fact that many distinguished Roman Catholic theologians as well as many less distinguished clergy and lay people see no reason why women should not be ordained into the priesthood of their Church. The lay Roman Catholic theologian Michael Novak has said that 'in some sense at the altar the priesthood of the Church needs fully to represent Christ and humanity both through male and female.' There is a growing movement in many parts of the Roman Catholic Church to promote this idea despite the refusal of the Vatican to open the subject for frank discussion.

If (or when) the Roman Catholic Church decides to admit women to the priesthood it will be taking a great risk. It may prove to be a risk of great benefit to the whole Church. Already people in the parishes are becoming accustomed to religious sisters and other women taking an increasing part in the Mass, including the administration of communion as well as leading prayers and reading the Scriptures. In its devotional life the Roman Catholic Church accords honour to the Virgin Mary in language appropriate to priesthood. When Pope John Paul II inaugurated the Marian year in 1987, he said:

> In the light of Mary the Church sees in the face of women the reflection of a beauty which mirrors the loftiest sentiments of which the human heart is capable: the self-offering totality of love: the strength which is capable of bearing the greatest sorrows: limitless fidelity and tireless devotion to work: the ability to combine penetrating intuition with words of support and encouragement.

In these words, obviously without recognising it, the Pope was giving a good job description for an ideal woman priest! When the Church of England ordains women it will give encouragement and support to those many Roman Catholics who risk disagreement with official Vatican policy by believing that sooner or later the ordination of women to the priesthood will be accepted in their own Church too.

When the General Synod was ready to proceed with the necessary legislation to enable women to become priests, there were threats of schism within the Church. Some priests were already considering joining the Roman Catholic Church or leaving the ministry altogether. In consequence it was agreed to soften the blow by certain compensatory regulations. When the measure became law, bishops already in post would be able to make a declaration, within six months, that no woman would be ordained priest in their diocese, or be instituted, licensed or given permission to officiate. Bishops appointed after the measure became law could not make such a declaration, but would not be obliged personally to ordain women into the priesthood, but would be in duty bound to make arrangements for another bishop to do so. Priests who felt in conscience that they had to resign would be given financial help in housing, and relocation, a resettlement grant, and would also receive monthly payments until eligible for a retirement pension.

The movement of clergy opposed to the ordination of women called itself 'The Cost of Conscience'. But these compensatory proposals showed that the Church of England was itself prepared to pay a considerable amount to cover the cost of the consciences of those not ready to accept her own democratically agreed decisions. Was this a splendid act of charity, or a ridiculous concession to what is likely to be a fairly small minority of rebels? It was a choice between two risks. Some dubbed the proposals the 'Thirty Pieces of Silver'. A layman, expressing disquiet at the whole business, said that Church members were being asked to hold bring-and-buy sales and bazaars to pay men not to continue as priests. Some saw the option given to bishops not to ordain women priests or appoint them, as a pandering to individual conscience. The Bishop of Durham was, as usual, more forthright: 'We have compromised ourselves by going along with the forms of legislation we now have. The compromise for us is the cost of conscience. Why should good, caring and conscientious priests, who many of us know, and many of us believe are mistaken in opposing the ordination of women, trouble the collective consciences more than the good, caring and conscientious women who are excluded from the ministry, and who are being treated more and more as pawns in a political game?'

When the Cameron Committee was already well advanced in its work it was forcibly faced with a new issue. In 1989 in the United States Episcopal Church, Barbara Harris was consecrated coadjutor Bishop of Massachusetts. A year later in New Zealand, Dr Penny Jamieson was consecrated Bishop of the Anglican diocese of Dunedin. The reality of two women bishops within the Anglican Communion added a new dimension to the Cameron deliberations on the episcopate. As they came to consider the matter they found that they were sharply divided along exactly the same lines as have marked the disagreement over women priests. They could detect no fresh theological reasons either for or against women bishops. They were certain that women bishops could not be justified simply by reference to the fact that women today frequently hold high positions of authority in secular institutions. They were also aware of the special role of bishops as a focus of unity. This pointed to the necessity of restraint in a single province of the Anglican Church in order to allow for wider participation in the decision-making process. But the Cameron group was quite unable to find a united theological criterion, and the pages of their report are peppered with such phrases as 'some of us thought' and 'others of us thought'. There was no other conclusion they could have reached except to disagree politely among themselves. They had to be content to put their disagreement into the wider context of ecumenical debate:

> From the beginning of the Church there have been strains on communion and breaks in communion. The modern ecumenical movement, with its attempt to re-establish ecclesial communion, has contributed the insight that, in spite of disagreements leading to divisions, the Christian Churches as they work towards unity still have much which binds them together in their common baptism and its implications; they are not 'in communion', but share a communion which is only partial. Moreover, in a divided Church, all ministry lacks the fullness which would pertain to a single ministry in a united Church, and may therefore in some sense be described as 'provisional'. The growing awareness in the whole ecumenical debate that we are not 'out of communion' with our brothers and sisters of other Churches is an important lesson to apply to the internal Anglican Communion and unity.[8]

Jesus taught that the kingdom of heaven is like a householder who brings out from his storeroom things both old and new. It is the task of the Church in each generation to hold the old and the new, not in a balance of easy compromise but in a difficult creative tension. Among all the acres of print devoted to the ordination of women, few wiser words were published than in a joint letter from the Superior General of the Society of St John the Evangelist and the Provincial of the Society of the Sacred Mission: 'We know that within our Societies there are those who support and those who oppose the ordination of women to the priesthood. There are those who think the subject is not one of major importance. However, we live and pray together, trying to respect and understand one another's position, but refusing to let the subject vitiate our work and witness.' Bishop David Hope spoke to the press in the same spirit when it was announced that he was to be the new Bishop of London. Because it was known that he was an opponent of the ordination of women, the media expected that his appointment would stir up fresh controversy. They were disappointed. His reply to a reporter's question revealed a humbler and more sensitive approach. He said frankly that he was not happy with the legislation then going through General Synod. He had hesitations and reservations about it: 'I am saddened by the confrontation which develops over this question, and before I cast my vote I still want to listen to the various opinions. It is important to listen even at this stage. I must remain open to the promptings of the Spirit.' As he prepared to move to a diocese deeply divided on this question he wanted to make it known that he hoped to be able to remain in communion with all his people, though there would be a great deal of pain on one side or other, whichever way the decision goes.

The last word on this subject can be given to a lawyer who in a cheeky letter to *The Times* asked, 'Is it at all appropriate, whilst the prelates are thwacking each other with their thuribles (oh so eirenically) to suggest that the sensible resolution of issues such as this one was that proposed by Gamaliel?' If it were not for Gamaliel's timely intervention in the Sanhedrin debate the young Church in Jerusalem might have died in infancy. 'If this enterprise, this movement of theirs, is of human origin it will break up of its own accord; but if it does in fact come from God you will not only be unable to destroy them, but you might find yourselves fighting against God.'[9]

This wise Pharisee knew from his Old Testament studies that the risk-taking God makes his purpose known through trial and error. Without the courage to take risks, the future remains unexplored and new truths remain hidden.

PRIESTLY LIFESTYLES

In the Church of England the shortage of candidates for the ministry and the difficulty of providing adequate staffing for the parishes has compelled a reconsideration of traditional styles of ministry and encouraged experiments in new directions. What began as a practical response to an emergency situation soon led to a recognition that there were profound questions about ministry and strategy to be asked. The role of non-stipendiary priests, the debate on the ordination of women to the priesthood, experiments in locally based ordained priests and the discovery of much more dynamic roles for lay women and men in ministry, were no longer seen as matters of 'bread and butter' administration. Theological questions about the nature of the Church itself were being raised. The risk-taking God was using the shortage of ministers to foment the beginning of a revolution in the Church. Instead of blandly praying for more ministers as the Church had bidden us to do, we were beginning to ask whether the short supply of clergy was part of a divine strategy to shake the Church out of a complacency lulled by long-standing accepted ways of running the ecclesiastical machine.

The Roman Catholic Church is now facing precisely the same challenge. In particular it is having to examine the relevance of the traditional priestly style to the contemporary situation, to ask whether the compulsory celibacy of the clergy is still of value and to take seriously the pressure from the laity to be liberated into a greater responsibility for shaping the faith and life of their Church. Because the Roman Catholic Church places such importance on the authority and tradition from which it gains so much of its strength, the risk-taking God may here be making even greater demands for change and facing tougher resistance from the traditionalists. In Britain the Roman Catholic Church has suffered a considerable decline in the number of men training for the priesthood during the past few decades when the total Catholic population and the number of parishes have increased. Vacancies on parish staffs are hard to fill, and the average age of the clergy increases annually. A similar situation faces the Church in most European countries and even more acutely in parts of North and South America. In some parts of the world one Catholic priest may be responsible for ministering to several thousand church members. For many of the faithful, opportunities for attending Mass and receiving communion are infrequent.

This drastic shortfall in the number of priests is partly due to the diminishing number of candidates entering the seminaries. In every diocese urgent appeals are made to parish congregations to do all that is in their power to foster vocations. But equally serious is the number of men who decide to leave the ministry within a few years of their ordination. The total number is reckoned to be 100,000 world-wide, nearly one quarter of active priests. Statistics are always open to question, but on any reckoning this is a critical situation. Men who renounce their priesthood do so for a variety of reasons. Some are unable to cope with celibacy, having reached the point when they make a clear decision to get married and embrace a family life. Some say that they find the clerical environment in which they must live claustrophobic. They feel that their priesthood traps their humanity. They are not at liberty to be their 'real selves'. Others come to resent the authoritarian style of the Church, feeling (rightly or wrongly) that the hierarchy is not sympathetic to those who are unwilling to accept the strict party line. If they have doctrinal or moral difficulties they feel they must keep quiet about them, suspecting that the Church wishes to hide from such truths. This adds up to the conviction that they have chosen the wrong job and should leave it to find an outlet more in tune with their personal needs and convictions. This failure of nerve among clergy, who are now ready to be more articulate about it, inevitably has an impact on young men who are considering training for the priesthood. They begin to doubt whether they can commit themselves for a lifetime to this kind of situation, especially as it involves an irrevocable decision to deny themselves the possibility of marriage and family life – or even normal relations with the opposite sex. Roman Catholic bishops write pastoral letters urging the faithful to pray for an increase in vocations. Some of the faithful believe that however important pastorals and prayers may be, there is an even greater urgency for an honest and profound examination of how the present situation came about and how it can be put right.

In October 1990 the bishops were summoned by Pope John Paul II to meet in solemn synod in Rome. The purpose of the meeting was to consider the formation and role of the priesthood today. Hopes were raised that they would examine and challenge the traditional ways of understanding priesthood in view of the cultural, pastoral and theological insights of the past two decades. The bishops last met in synod on this theme in 1971. Since then the second Vatican Council has initiated a movement in which the ordering of the Sunday liturgy has come to involve a variety of lay ministries. Other kinds of ministry have developed in such areas as peace and justice, ecumenism, and social responsibility. There are emerging many gifts of the Spirit appropriate to ministry which receive little official recognition but which impinge on an understanding of priesthood. Other questions have come to the fore which raised hopes for the 1990 Episcopal Synod. Would the bishops now consider lay ministry, priestly celibacy, the ordination of women? Although the preliminary documents were not received with great enthusiasm, they suggested that the synod would do this work fully conscious of the relevance of the secular context in which the priesthood must fulfil its mission. They spoke of pornography which ridiculed the virtues of chastity, virginity and celibacy. They saw the laudable concern for human rights, respect for women's place in society and attention to the environment contradicted by the individualism and subjectivism which lay at the door of many social evils. They deplored the empty enjoyment brought about by the misuse of drugs and alcohol. They acknowledged the moral challenge which comes from such technical advances as biogenetics and nuclear energy. They saw that for many people this advance brought about an agnosticism and neglect of religion leading to a new kind of paganism.

This diagnosis raised hopes that when the bishops talked together in this realistic context they would hear the risk-taking God calling them to discover new character studies and job descriptions to enable the priesthood to continue its traditional role but in tune with the kind of existence through which the people to whom they are called to minister have to live their lives. For many the messages which began to emerge from this month-long top-level consultation came as a disappointment. The bishops were clearly intent on maintaining the status quo rather than venturing into a risky future. Priestly precepts from the 1971 Synod were repeated with approval. Pastors of the Church were to excel in the witness of holiness. The identity of the priest was to live Christ's life, to live the gospel and to have a willing disposition towards mission, which are all grounded in the Eucharist, the heart of priestly spirituality. Their work demands an intense spiritual life until the summit of holiness is reached.

No one can criticise this splendid and pious definition except that to contemplate it must lead the average sensitive and conscientious parish priest to something like despair. He knows that he is not like that – he knows he is not a very effective icon of Christ, he knows that he does not excel in the witness of holiness, he knows that he has not reached 'the summit of holiness'. He does his work as faithfully as he can on the lower slopes. He knows with St Paul that all have sinned and come short of the glory of God, and he knows that 'all' includes not only the people to whom he ministers, but his bishops, his fellow priests and himself. He knows that the wonder of his calling to be a priest is that God knows the secrets of his heart and still accepts him just as he is, to be his minister. The bishops seem to have been more interested in reiterating the traditional ideas of priesthood, hardly attainable even among the saints, than in facing up to the practicalities of the hard slog which is demanded of the ordinary priest as he tries to do his job in his parish as faithfully as he can. If anyone needs to be persuaded that God is a risk-taker, he has only to look at the people he calls to be his agents. Many priests and faithful laity discover an exhilaration as they come to know themselves as part of God's risk-taking enterprise.

A major disappointment in the opinion of many was that the synod found nothing new to say about the celibacy of the priesthood. This is not surprising as the Pope had made it known that he did not want this on the agenda. Some bishops did their best to raise it, but the final Message read at the concluding Mass presented the traditional line couched in the language of Vatican-speak.

> Celibacy has shone out for us in a new light and with a new clarity. Celibacy is a complete self-giving to God for the good of souls: an intimate union with Christ the bridegroom who so loved his bride the Church that he gave up his life for her. Observing the evangelical counsels (chastity, poverty, and obedience) remains a sure way of acquiring virtue and attaining a true and complete freedom of Spirit.

Reading statements of this kind, married clergy in other Christian traditions might want to question whether priests who are celibate under compulsion are necessarily any more 'self-giving to God', 'in love with Christ' or 'acquire virtue and attain a true freedom of Spirit' than their fellow priests in other

Churches whose priestly vocation to serve God is no less seriously expressed in the state of marriage and the enjoyment of family life. It is tempting to ask whether the quasi-mystical statements on the necessity of celibacy which issue from the Vatican from time to time are written by men who not only have no first-hand experience of marriage, but who also have not had any serious conversation with married bishops and clergy in other Christian communions. Such statements seem to blur rather than elucidate the basic theological and pastoral issues involved.

There is no need to question the value of celibacy willingly undertaken in the fulfilment of priestly vocation. This has been the experience of many of the finest priests in the Church of England. Celibacy is seen as a gift from God gracefully offered and gratefully received by those who believe that this is the way God has called them to express their total availability to do the work to which Christ has ordained them. One Roman Catholic priest has said how his celibacy and his dedication to others 'sometimes makes him a silent yet challenging indictment to the selfishness of a secularised world'. But a married parish priest, faithful to his wife and family, can be a similar indictment to the selfishness which creates so much marital disruption today. Others have claimed that the celibate life rescues the priest from a bourgeois lifestyle. But some celibate presbyteries display as much addiction to bourgeois values as many vicarages – and may be none the worse for that! Arguments on either side of this question tend to cancel one another out. If celibacy is God's will for some of his priests (as surely it must be) here is a further sign of divine risk-taking. For the sexual instinct in men and women is a powerful one, not easily suppressed or sublimated. Ordination does not provide an inoculation against eroticism.

No discussion about celibacy can avoid the difficult questions about the way sexuality is approached in the formation of priests in the seminaries. Father Brian O'Sullivan has written:

> Wholeness must precede holiness if grace is to build on nature. The fact that so many priests have left the active ministry and married, and that many who have remained have experienced burn out or died prematurely, indicate that something was seriously wrong with their training . . .

In former times the requirement for ordination was to keep your head down and obey the rules. The training was excessively academic and nobody of the staff got to know the students. Emotion and sexuality were ignored, buried or sublimated.[10]

At their 1990 annual conference, meeting only a few days before the Bishops' Synod in Rome, the National Council for the Lay Apostolate discussed the formation of priests. They thought that seminaries seemed to be preoccupied with the cultivation of a priestly manner 'leading to the production of a caste rather than a brotherhood'. There should be much more utilisation of lay expertise in the training of priests, more consideration of sexuality and the use of 'excellent women spiritual directors now available'. They also declared that 'if the forthcoming Synod did not address the question of sexuality it would be omitting a vital matter'. The bishops did not take their advice. In one of the synodical documents it was stated that 'chastity in celibacy is not simply a juridical norm, not a totally external condition for being admitted to ordination, but a love for Christ and his Church. Celibacy presupposes an emotional maturity which is not easily attained.' Here there is no recognition that 'emotional maturity' can also be attained through marriage and family life. If this is so (and who can deny it?) is it not reasonable to believe that the God who took the risk of implanting sexuality within human experience also risks the use of this gift in his ministers through the free choice of 'maturing' either in celibacy or in marriage? Neither marriage nor celibacy is to be enforced. A gift is a gift, to be willingly both offered and accepted.

If, as seems certain, Scripture, theology and common sense are on the side of voluntary celibacy, why does the Roman Catholic hierarchy remain so opposed to it? To change an age-long tradition in the light of altered circumstances is always difficult. It suggests a weakening of authority. It might also weaken the centralised power that the bishops have over the clergy. Someone has described compulsory celibacy as 'the ultimate management technique, giving total control and total mobility of personnel'. But it is difficult to avoid the conclusion that it reflects a contorted view of human sexuality. Sexual intercourse as the means of procreation is obviously allowable, but in other respects it is suspect as leading to impurity. It is not for priests who celebrate the Mass to soil themselves by having sex with a woman – even a wife. This view dies hard as was illustrated in the recent *cause célèbre* of the two Brazilian married men who had been given special papal dispensation to become priests on condition that they lived with their wives 'only as brothers and sisters'. Commenting on this case, Dr Jack Dominian wrote: 'Either married Catholics in exceptional circumstances should be allowed to become priests while retaining their full married life in so far as they wish, or it should not be possible for them to be ordained. To ban co-habitation is a human and scriptural anomaly that no objective, even the safeguarding of priestly celibacy, can justify.'

Of the thousands of Roman Catholic priests who have resigned their priesthood, many claim to have taken this step because they longed for the companionship which marriage and family life could bring them, or because the celibate state was failing to meet their natural sexual needs. Training for their ordination may have started when they were in their teens, long before they had experienced the full force of sexual desire or falling in love. Warnings against establishing close relationships with women seemed reasonable until almost inadvertently such a relationship happened. Then celibacy vows became broken, inevitably clandestinely and with a growing sense of guilt. When the man eventually feels compelled to leave the priesthood in search of a more satisfactory way of life, the step is very costly and seldom lightly undertaken. There is a sense of personal failure, the hurt of distressing parents and friends, and a feeling of betraying the Church which has been his mother from early years. It is well known that some remain in the priesthood continuing in the active ministry with their sexual partners hidden from public view.

An important contribution to this debate comes from the experience of those married clergy who have left their own denomination to seek ordination in the Roman Catholic Church. A number of Church of England clergy have taken this step, or are contemplating it at the prospect of women being ordained in their own Church. Already in the 1960s Pope Pius XII authorised the ordination into the priesthood of some married convert Lutheran ministers in Germany. Paul VI also allowed the possibility of the ordination of 'married sacred ministers of Churches and other Christian communities separated from the Catholic Communion and to continue to exercise their sacred ministry'. Paul VI was known to have a deep affection for the Anglican Communion and during his pontificate four Anglican married priests were ordained in Australia (1969). It was not until 1983 that the Roman Catholic Bishops' Conference of England and Wales decided that 'the time is opportune for consideration of individual applications of married convert clergy for acceptance as candidates for the priesthood in the Catholic Church.'

To move from the Anglican to the Roman Catholic priesthood as a number of married priests have done in England poses many difficulties. By taking this step is the former Anglican denying the validity of his former ordination? 'I am not denying anything by my coming ordination,' wrote one such priest. 'I have never been asked to deny anything. I have, however, been welcomed in a truly generous way into the fullness of Catholicity which subsists in communion with the see of Rome. My Anglican heritage has always been respected and never disparaged.'

How will a Catholic congregation accustomed to a celibate parish priest welcome the ministry of a married man with a wife in the presbytery? This question has not yet been put to the test in England. Married convert priests have not been given parochial charge. Instead they are appointed as chaplains to hospitals, prisons, schools, colleges or working with Catholic charities. Father Michael Gaine, secretary of the Movement for the Ordination of Married Men says about the English situation, 'It looks as though the existence of married priests is to be treated as a slightly guilty secret in our midst rather than being celebrated as a positive development in the life of the Church.' Where elsewhere convert married priests have been appointed to parishes there has been no indication of special difficulties. Writing of their experiences in Australia, a former Anglican priest says on behalf of his colleagues in a similar situation that 'our experience has shown that not only do the Catholics accept married priests as their pastors, they warmly welcome him and his wife and family in their midst.'

Those married clergy who move over to Rome from a ministry in other Churches are not simply honouring their own consciences, they are making a pioneer contribution to the development of the Church they have joined by giving parishes the experience of discovering what it is like to have a married priest for a pastor. At the same time, many leading Roman Catholic theologians have been working on the much-neglected theology of sexuality, and this may serve to banish some of the out-of-date fears about sexual emotions which have a place (consciously or unconsciously) in the continuing insistence on the upholding of compulsory celibacy. The need for more open and frank dialogue between celibate and married ministries could help to expel the myths each may have about the other. If carried on with mutual respect and harmony on an ecumenical basis among ordained ministers in their own locality, this could provide a fruitful opportunity for 'correction of one another in Christ'. Those who have the courage to share openly in this kind of dialogue may find that they have to manoeuvre round some dangerous corners as inner anxieties are brought to the surface and familiar stereotypes are challenged. There can be no way forward until such risks are taken in faithful response to the promptings of the risk-taking God.

7

ECUMENISM

INTER-CHURCH

THE CHRISTIAN CHURCH makes the bold claim that it
has been created by God to bring healing and reconciliation
to a divided world. It has been singularly unsuccessful in practising what it preaches. Christians remain sadly divided as between
one denomination and another, and even within the separate
traditions. When people come out from their own churches on
rare occasions to join in a united service, they sing with great
gusto and confidence:

> We are not divided,
> All one body we,
> One in hope and doctrine,
> One in charity.

– words which are manifestly untrue. When Anglicans go to
Holy Communion, at a key moment in the service they proclaim
in the words of St Paul: 'We break this bread to share in the
body of Christ. Though we are many we are one body because
we share in the same bread.' If they paused for a moment to
think what they were saying, they would remember that not all
Christians share in the same bread. Some of them would not
be willing to go to the Breaking of Bread in a Baptist chapel,
and few non-Catholics would be welcome if they presented
themselves for communion at the local Roman Catholic Church.
The bread of the Universal Church has been tragically broken,
and there is a reluctance amongst many worshippers to do
anything about it. The twentieth century has sometimes been
heralded as the 'century of ecumenism'. There has been no

lack of resounding proclamations, carefully prepared reports and unity schemes. Modest experiments have been tried: a few have succeeded. But again and again splendid proposals have failed at the last moment. The Churches have been frightened to take the required steps because they do not dare risk bringing about the death of their own much-loved tradition in the interests of a greater unity.

In Britain the last hundred years have told a frustrating story of hopes for real progress in unity raised, then dashed, then raised again. The final decade of the present century finds the British Churches in a mood of hopefulness tinged with nagging anxiety and no little cynicism.

Archbishop William Temple was enthroned in Canterbury Cathedral when the world was deeply divided by war and the very independence of the United Kingdom was threatened by severe bombardment from the air and the fear of a German invasion from across the Channel. In his sermon he chose to speak of the world-wide task of the Church:

> As though in preparation for such a time as this, God has been building up a Christian fellowship which now extends into almost every nation, and binds citizens of them all together in true unity and mutual love. No human agency has planned this. It is the result of the great missionary enterprise of the last hundred and fifty years. Neither the missionaries nor those who sent them out were aiming at a world-wide fellowship interpenetrating the nations, bridging the gulfs between them and supplying the promise of a check on their rivalries. The aim for nearly the whole period was to preach the gospel to as many individuals as could be reached so that those who were won to discipleship should be put in the way of eternal salvation. Almost incidentally the great world fellowship has arisen: it is the great new fact of our time.[1]

This was a magnificent vision proclaimed in 1942 from the pulpit of the central church of the Anglican communion while the nations were waging a terrible war. How true do those words ring fifty years later? Has the vision faded?

Temple knew that the world-wide task given to the Church

to bring reconciliation and healing to a war-torn world could only be achieved if Christians worked towards a closer unity among themselves. In 1942, largely through his towering influence, the British Council of Churches came into being. When the World Council of Churches was formed six years later William Temple had already been dead for four years. He had not lived to see the formation of the world ecumenical body which was his dream and largely his creation. The question can never be answered whether the ecumenical movement would have moved faster and to greater purpose if Temple had lived. The World Council of Churches continues its difficult task, organising many important meetings, publishing significant reports, and issuing huge quantities of paper, with an influence scarcely commensurate with its weight. After forty years of hard work, involving many prominent Church leaders and thinkers, clerical and lay, the British Council of Churches went out of existence in the summer of 1990. It has given place to the new British 'ecumenical instrument' whose worth is yet to be proved. Its greater promise lies in the fact that a risk element appears to have been written into its constitution. It is a pilgrimage and not a blueprint.[2]

It must be hoped that all the energy and disappointment of this ecumenical century now in its closing years will provide the soil for significant growth in the century ahead. Past experience provides many lessons and warnings. The modern ecumenical movement was born out of the great missionary enterprise of the last century. Its birth date is often given as 1910, when the International Missionary Council held a world-wide conference in Edinburgh to consider how the missionary work of the Church was often frustrated and compromised by divisions among Christians. William Temple was a student usher at the conference and it deeply influenced his whole life. Also involved were other world bodies, notably the Student Christian Movement and the Young Men's Christian Association. These later provided many young men and women to become leaders in the World Council of Churches and in their own denominations. Amongst these young Christians was often heard the slogan 'The Evangelisation of the World in our Generation'. It is doubtful whether many now involved in the Decade of Evangelism are motivated by such an ambitious and optimistic objective.

It was a risky vision, but it attracted some of the best minds among the younger Church leaders of that time.

A more cynical generation lay ahead. As the century progressed, the ecumenical movement became more preoccupied with the mechanics of ecclesiastical joinery than with world mission. Ecumenism came to mean 'being nice' to members of other Churches, with occasional joint services, joint protests about things they could all disapprove (some Christians are never happier than joining in a protest or signing a petition), and (less often) some joint action on a worthy cause. Local Councils of Churches, which began to be formed in the 1940s and 1950s and were initially rather exciting and risky ventures, soon began to lose their initiative, because they came to be inward-looking, self-satisfied and parochial. They lost their cutting edge because they failed to grasp the wider vision which inspired the founders of the modern ecumenical movement who spoke of their vision as the proclamation of the whole gospel by the whole Church to the whole world. The awful crime came to be committed of making the ecumenical movement boring.

It is not surprising that the most significant venture in ecumenism in Britain in this century has been Christian Aid, which invites both churchgoers and the wider public to stop thinking about themselves and their local concerns and see that a practical response to the desperate needs of two-thirds of our fellow inhabitants of the globe is not an optional interest for Christians, but an essential element in the preaching of the gospel of Jesus Christ. Christian Aid is an important element in the ecumenical movement because it is organised by the Churches working together to make available practical aid which is normally distributed by Christians working together in the areas of need. It is totally ecumenical, both at the giving and receiving end. Christian Aid knows that much of its work involves risk when political judgements have to be made on unjust governments which repress their people and so carry responsibility for the poverty, injustice and discrimination which dehumanises them. In the difficult work of world development Christian workers know that unless they are prepared to take risks there can be no progress. In this light, it is fair to ask why it is that the denominations here at home are so unwilling to take the risks which could break down many of the barriers which separate them, and liberate them to work more effectively for mission and service to their own country.

This is a question which has often been asked. Answers are less in evidence. In 1952 eighty distinguished theologians from many Churches and many parts of the world met for ten days in the Swedish university city of Lund, to talk together about the things that hinder and the things that promote Christian unity. Their report, now sadly neglected, was a significant call to divided Churches to discover the urgency of the movement towards Christian unity in the broken post-war world. They knew that there could be no such movement until the Churches realised that complacency must give place to urgency, playing safe must give place to risk-taking and ecclesiastical self-satisfaction must yield to self-sacrifice. The message they sent to the Churches still has great power.

> Those who are ever looking backward and have accumulated much precious ecclesiastical baggage will perhaps be shown that pilgrims must travel light and that, if we are to share at the last great supper, we must let go much that we treasure. Churches settled and self-assured will have to hear again the Lord's heart-broken concern for the sheep without a shepherd and to know that to be his Church is to share in his world-embracing mission. Churches too much at home in the world will hear themselves called out of the world. Churches too wrapped up in their own piety or their own survival will see again Him who identified Himself with the deprived and the oppressed. We cannot know all that shall be disclosed to us when together we look to Him who is the Head of the body. It is easy for us in our several Churches to think of what our separated brethren need to learn. Christ's love will make us more ready to learn what He can teach us through them.

This led them to ask the central question which is still called, by those who remember it, the Lund Principle: 'Should not our Churches ask themselves whether the time has come when they should act together in all matters, except those in which deep differences of conviction compel them to act separately?'

Between 1942 and 1990 the Churches of Great Britain (with the exception of the Church of Rome) had a focus of unity as members of the British Council of Churches. Their leading churchmen and women frequently met on its proliferating councils and committees. They came to know each other, generally to trust one another, and many became personal friends. Archbishop Fisher succeeded Temple as the Council's president and, in spite of a rather headmasterly style, commanded a wide degree of respect and affection. He felt that some initiative was required from him to break the deadlock in which the divided Churches in Britain found themselves. He was convinced that it was the failure to give full recognition to one another's ministries which lay at the heart of the problem. Anglicans were unable to accept the validity (whatever that word means) of holy orders which are not episcopally transmitted through the so-called apostolic succession. The Free Churches, understandably, refused to enter into any scheme which cast doubt on the adequacy of their existing ministries. Fisher thought that as the Methodists, Congregationalists and Baptists already had district chairmen or other appointed officers exercising some kind of oversight or *episcope*, it would be a comparatively small step for them to take 'episcopacy into their system'. Once that step was taken it would not be too difficult to move forward together into intercommunion and eventual union. Without denying Fisher's *bona fide*, the Free Churches had their suspicions aroused. Was episcopacy really a necessary condition for intercommunion? The Free Churches celebrated Holy Communion together without bothering about bishops! Anyhow, what kind of episcopacy was the Church of England trying to impose on them? They knew well that Anglicans held a number of different views on the nature of the episcopal office. Were they being cajoled into accepting a concept of episcopacy which they suspected was unbiblical? But the most serious objection to the Fisher scheme was that he appeared to be inviting the Free Churches to undertake considerable changes themselves while the Church of England would remain exactly as it had been. If, as is inevitable in any unity scheme, risks had to be taken, it was not the Anglican Church which had any intention of taking them.

Nine years later the Methodist Church responded by resolving that it should enter into conversations with the Church of

England in order to promote intercommunion between the two Churches along the lines suggested by the archbishop. But before conversations could begin, the Methodists very wisely insisted on three provisos. One: that the Church of England must make clear that our divisions are within the Christian body; there must be no suggestion that this was a means by which the Methodists would be brought back into the true Church. Two: the same liberty of interpretation of the nature of priesthood and episcopacy should be accorded to the Methodist Church as already prevailed in the Church of England. Three: that the Methodist Church would be free to preserve intercommunion and fellowship with other non-episcopal Churches which it then enjoyed.

A joint commission of the two Churches was set up in 1956 to prepare a unity scheme. It reported in 1963. They had found a genuine agreement between the two Churches on the authority of Scripture and tradition, on the basic teachings of the gospel, on Church order, ministry and sacraments. There was enough agreement between them to bring forward specific proposals for unity for consideration by the two governing bodies, allowing a three-year period for discussion not only centrally but in dioceses, districts, deaneries, circuits and local congregations. Final decisions would not be taken until substantial groundwork and preparation had been undertaken by the two Churches at every level. Only then would they be ready to invite one another to take the necessary risks.

It was an imaginative scheme, envisaging a two-stage process. First the Churches would enter into a period of full intercommunion and integration of ministries without yet becoming one Church. This first stage would be achieved by a mutual recognition and uniting of ministries by prayer and laying-on of hands. This would be followed by area services and the consecration of Methodist bishops elected by the Methodist conference. All subsequent ordinations would be by bishops and other ministers. This first stage, which might last ten or even twenty years, would lead to the full union of the two Churches after the complex legal and administrative procedures had been completed. It was agreed that each Church must take a final vote of at least seventy per cent in favour in order to signify that it was ready to proceed to the first stage of the scheme. Both

Churches voted simultaneously on the same day. The Methodists achieved a 78 per cent vote. The Church of England failed
to obtain the necessary majority. So the scheme fell to the
ground. When the General Synod voted again two years later,
the same negative result was obtained. Many people in both
Churches felt bitterly disappointed that such a hopeful opportunity for a great step forward in unity between two leading
British Churches was thrown away. Archbishop Michael
Ramsey told his fellow bishops: 'We Anglicans have liked to
think of ourselves as being the leaders in the matter of Christian
unity. But at the moment we are not: it is the Methodists who
are leaders now.' It is said that the failure of the Anglican-
Methodist scheme was for Michael Ramsey the most disappointing moment of his life.[3]

This book is about the risk-taking God, and the essential
place of risk in the life of his Church. The failure of the
Anglican-Methodist scheme provides a valuable object lesson
on this theme. The plan was designed with an in-built risk
element. It included many unresolved ambiguities, particularly
in relation to the episcopate. It left open certain questions about
the requirements of faith and order necessary to provide a stable
unity. It envisaged a lengthy period after initial commitment for
a process of growing together in which trial and error would
have a place. It was this risky uncertainty which contributed to
the scheme's rejection. Those who wanted a unity based on
hard-and-fast lines would have nothing to do with its vagueness.
To the anglo-catholics it was playing fast and loose with the
sacred traditions 'once delivered to the saints'. To the evangelicals it invited a mistaken understanding of the will of God
revealed in Scripture. Not for the first (nor last) time a curious
alliance of 'high' and 'low' would not allow the majority in both
Churches to embark on a risky adventure. For the majority in
both Churches who were willing to accept the proposals, the
element of risk seemed a sign that they were ready to venture
into the unknown at the promptings of the Holy Spirit.

This disappointing failure had an influence which was not
entirely negative. There followed a steady rise in local ecumenical activity: Councils of Churches, joint neighbourhood study
groups, social action and shared services of Holy Communion.
Christian Aid not only grew into a major world-development

and emergencies agency, but drew together thousands of Christians of different denominations to work on behalf of the world's poor. The disillusionment about grandiose national schemes stimulated ecumenical work at the grass roots level. When ecumenism is accompanied by a sense of adventure and of breaking new ground, it generates enthusiasm and is able to move forward. But when it becomes a habit – a normal part of the church programme – the ecumenical movement ceases to move. Councils of Churches, local ecumenical projects, united study and witness, which seem to be so exciting and challenging in their early stages, quickly run out of steam. Enthusiasm wavers. Momentum is lost. Daring and imaginative plans degenerate into run-of-the-mill items on a dull church agenda. So ecumenism becomes a bore and a chore – a dead horse which a few remaining enthusiasts attempt to flog back into life. As soon as the ecumenical endeavour ceases to take risks, it loses power and sinks into inertia.

Even before the failure of the Anglican-Methodist scheme, five hundred delegates from all the main Churches in Great Britain, including observers from the Roman Catholic Church, had met in Nottingham for the first British Faith and Order Conference (1964). Participants came with a wide vision and were filled with enthusiasm. They issued a daring invitation to the Churches to take risks for the sake of unity. They offered a specific challenge tied to a definite date. They urged the member Churches of the British Council of Churches, in appropriate groups such as nations, to covenant together to work and pray for the inauguration of union by a date to be agreed among them. 'We dare to hope that this date should not be later than Easter Day 1980. We believe that we should offer obedience to God in a commitment as decisive as this.'

Ten years after Nottingham it was the United Reformed Church which took the initiative. As the only significant union of two separate denominations it had the right to urge its fellow Christians into action. A Christian Unity Commission was set up to include representatives of the Church of England, Baptists, Moravians, Roman Catholics, Methodists, Churches of Christ and the United Reformed Church itself. The Commission issued Ten Propositions which it was hoped the Churches would accept as a reasonably agreed basis upon which they could move forward together into unity. There was much discussion and innumerable pieces of paper were passed back and forth. But one by one the Churches rejected the scheme or, at best, were ready to accept it half-heartedly. The Baptists rejected it because it threatened their independence and because it threw into question their particular emphasis on the baptism of believers. The Roman Catholics rejected it as having a deficient concept of priesthood, nor could they accept immediate intercommunion, or the idea that each participating Church could be afforded equal status in the Holy Catholic Church. The Anglicans rejected it (on a majority negative vote by the clergy) on many of the same grounds on which the Methodist scheme had been rejected earlier. There was an additional worry in some quarters about entering into unity with those Free Churches which already had women ministers. The Methodists said they would come in if the Anglicans agreed to do so. The United Reformed Church was ready to accept the Ten Propositions if the recommendations about episcopacy would be clarified. Once again a unity scheme, promoted with much thought and devotion, collapsed. Once again it was the fear of taking risks and venturing into the unknown which caused another failure to get the unity movement in Britain off the ground. At the level of the local churches, the clergy and their congregations still had not come to know one another well enough to trust one another to take risks and to go forward together into God's unknown future.

In recent years the entry of the Roman Catholic Church upon the ecumenical scene has added new opportunities – and new problems – for progress in Christian unity in Britain. History may prove the Roman Catholic presence in the ecumenical movement in the last years of the twentieth century to be the factor above all others which rescued the Anglicans and the Free Churches from the stalemate and disenchantment which followed the collapse of so many unity schemes. Already in many areas the Roman Catholics are playing a major role in local Councils of Churches and ecumenical study and activities. Books by Roman Catholic theologians are being widely read and discussed beyond the membership of their own communion. The close partnership in ministry, mission and social concern between Archbishop Derek Warlock and Bishop David Sheppard, the Roman Catholic and Anglican Church leaders in Liverpool, has attracted widespread interest and appreciation. The steady work of the Anglican-Roman Catholic International Commission, with its agreed statements on Eucharistic doctrine, Ministry and Ordination, Authority in the Church and Salvation, may have attracted less public interest but has proved to be a valuable foundation upon which a growing understanding between Rome and Canterbury can be built. Whether real progress can be made will depend on whether both Churches will be prepared to take risks without appearing too obviously to be doing so.

The significant arrival of Rome on the ecumenical scene brings with it many problems. Anglicans and Free Churchmen who value the freedom from the control of the hierarchy which the Reformation gave them, are not willing to take the risk of having to believe and do unacceptable things which reunion with Rome might involve. Roman Catholics are worried that closer relations with the Churches of the Reformation might weaken the authority which their Church believes to be essential if there is to be unity of faith and practice. They find endless discussions amongst non-Catholics about the meaning and practice of the Eucharist, the virgin birth and the ordination of women to the priesthood, a sure sign that here are Christians who do not know what to believe because there is no ultimate authority to guide them. Anglicans feel insulted because the papal declaration *Apostolicae Curae* of 1896 declaring Anglican orders invalid is still in force. In 1950 the Assumption of the Blessed Virgin Mary was promulgated as an official dogma in the Roman Catholic Church and many Anglicans and Free Churchmen see this as making an even wider gap between the Churches.

When Archbishop Fisher went to Rome in 1960 to meet Pope John XXIII conditions were laid down that the meeting should be entirely private with no press reports. Afterwards Fisher told how the Pope had talked of his hope that the time would come when 'our separated brethren would return to Mother Church'. Fisher replied, 'Your Holiness, not "return".' 'Why not?' asked the Pope, and the Archbishop explained, 'None of us can go backward. We are each now running on parallel courses. We are looking forward until, in God's good time, our two courses approximate and meet.' The Pope then paused and said, 'You are right.' But it must have seemed a risky idea to the holy John XXIII. He had never before encountered an episcopal headmaster.[4]

Thirty years after that encounter Archbishop Runcie went to Rome to talk with Pope John Paul II. This encounter was accompanied by a blaze of publicity and much press and ecclesiastical speculation whether any good would come of it. The fact that in some parts of the Anglican Communion (though not in the Church of England) women had been ordained to the priesthood, caused grave forebodings that the meeting would be a failure. In their joint declaration the Pope and Archbishop did not dodge the issue: 'The question and practice of the admission of women to the ministerial priesthood in some provinces prevents reconciliation between us even where there is otherwise progress towards agreement in faith on the meaning of the Eucharist and the ordained ministry.' In the past such differences had been disguised behind the unclarity of ecclesiastical diplomatic jargon. The fact that they took the risk of coming out in the open in plain language on this disagreement was in itself a notable sign of ecumenical progress. It was a risky thing to do and the press responded by putting as pessimistic a gloss upon it as possible. Less notice was taken of the warmth with which John Paul II received his Anglican visitors and of the positive note struck by their final joint statement: 'We solemnly recommitted ourselves to the restoration of visible unity and full ecclesial communion in the confidence that to seek anything less would be to betray our Lord's intention for the unity of his people.'

In 1982 Pope John Paul II came to England. The visit was accounted a great success and the television pictures of His Holiness sharing in ecumenical worship in the Anglican cathedrals of Canterbury and Liverpool inspired many to believe that a new age of Christian unity was dawning. Ten years later these high hopes have diminished. Cheering crowds along the papal route and enthusiastic congregations in great cathedrals are no substitute for the tough realities which have to be faced and the risks which must be taken on all sides if the barriers which divide Christians from one another are finally to be done away.

The realisation in the 1980s that the British Council of Churches was beginning to outlive its usefulness opened up possibilities of new initiatives. Although the Roman Catholic Church had been willing to send observers to the Council and had followed its proceedings with close interest, it steadfastly refused to enter into its membership. In 1987, for the first time, representatives from all the Christian Churches in Great Britain and Ireland met in Swanwick to formulate future policy. In a historic declaration those present committed their Churches to take the risk of moving together into the unknown future as pilgrims sharing a journey together.[5] They determined to move from co-operation to a clear commitment to each other to search urgently for the unity for which Christ prayed in the common task of evangelism and service to the world. 'Our earnest desire', they pledged, 'is to become more fully, in his own time, the one Church of Christ, united in faith, communion, pastoral care and mission.'

Already in September 1990 separate Ecumenical Councils for England, Scotland, Wales and Ireland were established with much blowing of trumpets, expectant prayers, and belief that a great new chapter was being written in the story of Christianity in Britain. The emphasis is on pilgrimage. If it is to succeed the Churches must enter into a commitment with one another extending far beyond anything that has gone before. As Archbishop John Habgood wrote:

> This requires a shift in the thinking, feeling and actions of our Churches from an ecumenism which is an extra which absorbs energy to an ecumenism as a dimension of all that we do, which releases energy through the sharing of resources. This shift needs to be effective at all levels and in all places in order to establish a radically new style of working which builds on the creative ecumenical relationships of the many rather than the ecumenical activities of the few.[6]

Will the enthusiasm for this fresh start eventually run into the sands of inertia as has happened time and again in ecumenical enterprises during the past century? Will the massive involvement of the Roman Catholic Church hasten the ecumenical process, or slow it down? Will the charismatic movement, with its lack of interest in the institutional side of church life, prove a diversion from the major objectives of the new 'ecumenical process'? The answers to these, and many other questions, depend on enough historical sense and honesty to learn lessons from the past. The seeds of failure lie in the unwillingness of church members to sacrifice some of their cherished theological and ecclesiastical vested interests, and to jeopardise the familiar certainties of their own particular religious institution. Risk is an essential factor in the ecumenical adventure. Refusal to take risks leads to stalemate. The Churches cannot draw closer to one another without speaking the truth in complete honesty to one another, with readiness to learn from one another, and the daring to be honest with themselves. Only in that spirit can they explore and move forward together.

INTERCOMMUNION

In the summer of 1960 over a thousand young people from member Churches of the World Council of Churches came to the Swiss city of Lausanne for a European Assembly of Christian Youth. Because the various traditions represented – Orthodox, Lutheran, Anglican, Reformed – held different views about open communion, it was decided that there should be no celebration of Holy Communion for the whole Assembly. Each separate tradition could organise a Eucharistic service as required by its own members. This was a difficult and uncomfortable decision, but ecclesiastical policy and courtesy made it necessary. Half-way through the Assembly this decision was effectively sabotaged by one of the main invited speakers. Hans Hoekendijk, distinguished Dutch professor of Mission, urged his young audience to be impatient and do 'the impossible thing' by disregarding their confessional loyalty. There could be no movement in ecumenism unless people were ready to step out of their traditions. He spoke of the 'impossible thing' of intercommunion:

> I remember that in the history of the last 150 years many things have been considered impossible until they were

done. At first we thought we could not pray together. Then we could not come together in an inter-denominational conference without being a nuisance. Then we could not attend worship in each others churches. Impossible! Until it happened. I have the deep conviction that the Lord's Table is the place where we have to do the impossible now. And why not? It is the very place where all of us are invited.

The impact of this challenge was instantaneous. Within hours an 'unofficial' intercommunion service was organised, technically 'off' the conference programme. But over a thousand young people attended the service and received the sacrament together. For many it was the high point of the Assembly. This experience had an undoubted influence on many responsible young people who have since become leaders in their respective Churches.

In September 1972 five hundred leading representatives of the British and Irish Churches met for a ten-day consultation in Birmingham. Among the speakers was Cardinal Heenan, then Archbishop of Westminster. In the questions following his address he was asked whether non-Catholics might before long be allowed to receive communion in the Roman Catholic Church. His reply was that this could only happen in the most exceptional circumstances. When pressed to say what these 'exceptional circumstances' might be, he answered, 'Maybe in a concentration camp'. The chairman, Bernard Pawley, a noted Anglican student of Roman Catholic affairs, could not resist the interjection, 'It seems to me that we should pray for a multiplication of concentration camps' – a remark which caused much laughter in the auditorium but left the Cardinal looking somewhat discomforted.[7]

At the Roman Catholic Pastoral Congress in Liverpool in 1980 voices were heard raising the same question. Has not the time come when Roman Catholics and devout members of other Christian traditions should be permitted to express their faith in Christ together by sharing in the Eucharist? In their reflections on the Congress the Roman Catholic bishops gave the same answer that Cardinal Heenan had given in Birmingham eight years earlier. 'In certain circumstances for serious reasons the practice of admitting non-Catholics to Holy Communion has been allowed by the Universal Church when, for a considerable period, non-Catholics have no access to their own Church or minister, or when their faith in the Real Presence is compatible with our own. Such conditions would seem to be rarely fulfilled in our own countries.'[8] Shades of Cardinal Heenan's concentration camp!

Now that Roman Catholics have entered fully into the ecumenical partnership the question of intercommunion is certain to become more acute. The modern Eucharistic liturgy in English in use in Roman Catholic Churches is scarcely distinguishable from Rite A in the Church of England Alternative Services Book or contemporary Eucharistic rites in the Methodist, United Reformed and other Churches. If we use more or less the same words when we come to the Lord's Table, why should we not receive the sacrament together? The Pastoral Congress assertion that a further necessity for intercommunion is that we all have a compatible faith in the Real Presence is less convincing in the light of the rich diversity of Eucharistic theologies shared by Roman Catholics and non-Catholic scholars alike.

The official Roman Catholic view is that intercommunion cannot be justified as the means of achieving the ultimate goal of unity. It can only make sense when it is a sure sign that unity has already been achieved. The bishops in the Pastoral Congress report were clear on this point: 'In our present circumstances it is necessary to realise that it could be counter-productive to use what is the perfect symbol of unity as a means of achieving it. This could defer indefinitely the full corporate union for which we all pray.'[9]

In the 1990 meeting of the General Assembly of the Church of Scotland there was a strong majority vote in favour of asking the Roman Catholic Church in Scotland if a special dispensation could be granted to Catholic priests on ecumenical occasions 'to invite communicant members of all Churches present to come forward to the Lord's Table'. A minister from Aberdeen opposed the motion, arguing that 'the pain of being separated at the Eucharist represented the truth of the relationship between the two Churches and that to remove it on certain occasions of ecumenical joy and celebration would be ultimately frivolous.'

The question of intercommunion cannot be treated as an

unimportant side-issue to be conveniently ignored. It will have an increasingly central part in the ecumenical debate. There is no simple solution which can be easily accepted by all parties. It is a problem fraught with risk, and ultimate solutions will not be achieved without taking risks. Must Christians have a common agreement about the nature of the Church, the meaning of the Eucharist and the authority of ministers before they can join together at the Lord's Table? Must intercommunion always be seen as the certain mark of unity already achieved, or can it be with equal integrity a solemn token of a shared intention to move together to a unity which lies ahead? Is the pain of being separated at the Holy Communion a spur to fresh endeavour to work for unity or is it a kind of romantic self-indulgence ministering to the spiritual pride of those who wish to remain separated from the others?

In the autumn of 1990 the Roman Catholic weekly journal *The Tablet* printed a letter strongly advocating open communion. Its writer was Father Michael Simpson, a Jesuit priest of the St Beuno's Spiritual Exercise Centre in North Wales.[10] The letter, and the long correspondence to which it gave rise, illustrated the many facets of this serious matter. Father Simpson said that he had recently been invited to be celebrant at a Mass for a gathering which, while mostly Roman Catholic, would include Christians of other traditions. He knew that a notice would be read out following the instructions of the local diocese, saying that according to the discipline of the Church we would be unable to invite those who are not Roman Catholics to receive communion. 'For a number of years this issue has been causing me grievous unease. I am unable in conscience to celebrate Mass where this discipline is imposed.' He then gave three reasons for his unease. The first was to ask whether the question of who may validly minister the Eucharist must be closely identified with the question of who may rightly receive communion at a Eucharistic celebration.

> At the Last Supper only Jesus had the power and authority to institute the Eucharist and to minister at its celebration. But his sacred body and blood was offered to all the disciples, a group of weak, misunderstood and sinful men who had not yet been formed into an ecclesial community. It

would be the Eucharist that would help them into such a community.

Father Simpson sees that it is important to preserve the tradition that the Eucharist can only be celebrated by the sacramental community of faith through the hands of one ordained within the community to preside at its Eucharistic celebration and who embodies in this ministry the priestly power and authority given by Christ to the community, i.e., the Church. But he doubts the truth that the Eucharist is the symbol of belonging to the particular ecclesial community which celebrates it. The question of who may be allowed to receive is different from who may be allowed to minister.

> The meaning of the Eucharist is Christ who gives his body broken for all, and his blood shed for all. The Eucharist does not signify primarily what we do or what we are: it is the expression of God's mercy and love for all creation. It only signifies who we are in the sense of who we become in receiving his gift, namely his living body on earth, and this transcends the limits of ecclesial communion and divisions.

He quotes the Eucharist prayer, 'We offer you his body and his blood, the acceptable sacrifice which brings salvation to the whole world', commenting that it is contradictory to recite these words in the name of Christ, and then refuse to offer Christ's gift freely to those who come in sincerity of heart to receive. He then proceeds to comment on the assumption that the Eucharist is the expression of unity already attained rather than the means by which this unity will come about. He finds this view contradicted by many of the liturgical prayers in the Eucharist itself: 'May all of us who share in the body and blood of Christ be brought together in unity by the Holy Spirit.' And, 'Grant that we who are nourished by his body and blood may be filled with his Holy Spirit and become one body, one spirit.' Does this not identify the Church with Christ as his body is broken, and that it is through the Eucharist that it will be united? So Father Simpson declares the Eucharist to be for the unity, renewal, and mission of the Church, witnessing to the all-encompassing love of God:

In my view the discipline which refuses to invite those who recognise the presence of Christ in the Eucharist and who sincerely desire to feed on his body and to drink his blood, to share the divine gift with us is inherently sinful. This is both because it conflicts with the mind and heart of Jesus as revealed in the Gospel who offers his body and blood to all who will receive and because it reinforces the alienations and brokenness within the body, i.e., the Church, for which the Eucharist is precisely God's gift to bring healing, reconciliation and unity.

It is no surprise that such a clear departure from what is generally taken as the accepted Roman Catholic line should have led to a flood of letters both of criticism and approval. Typical of the former was a correspondent who insisted that the Eucharist as a symbol of belonging to an ecclesial community must for Catholics mean the Church, Holy, Roman, Catholic and Apostolic, because this is the ecclesial community *par excellence*, and to receive communion in that community implies accepting all the other doctrines defined at Trent regarding the Holy Sacrifice. A similar view was expressed by a writer who said that the Roman Catholic Church was 'already "one church" and that the prayers for unity in the liturgy were simply pleading for even more of a good thing already had'. Although Father Simpson stipulates that communion at Mass should be open to those 'who come in sincerity of heart to receive', some correspondents thought that this opened the door to an invitation to anyone to come in, willy nilly. Was the Sacrament to be offered to those who had not been confirmed, or even to the unbaptised, or to people who could not profess the historic creeds? Could this not lead to indifferentism, to a slipshod understanding of the Church and the Sacraments, or to no understanding at all?

Bishop Alan Clark, a leading Roman Catholic ecumenist, warned of the danger of vague statements about the meaning of the Real Presence of Christ in the Mass. He referred to the statements on the Eucharist in the report of the Anglican-Roman Catholic International Commission (ARCIC). The report stated that 'through the prayer of thanksgiving, a word of faith addressed to the Father, the bread and wine become the body and blood of Christ by the action of the Holy Spirit, so that in communion we eat the flesh of Christ and drink his blood.' This doctrine was expanded in the Elucidation:

> *Becoming* does not here imply material change. Nor does the liturgical use of the word imply that the bread and wine become Christ's body and blood in such a way that in the eucharistic celebration his presence is limited to the consecrated elements. It does not imply that Christ becomes present in the Eucharist in the same manner as he was present in his earthly life. It does not imply that this *becoming* follows the physical laws of this world. What is here affirmed is a sacramental presence in which God uses realities of the world to convey the realities of the new creation; bread from this life becomes the bread of eternal life. Before the Eucharistic prayer, to the question 'What is that?' the believer answers 'It is bread'. After the Eucharistic prayer, to the same question he answers 'It is truly the body of Christ, the Bread of Life'.[11]

Bishop Clark believes that only with an agreement on a statement of faith along these lines can there be an acceptable basis for intercommunion. 'The Eucharist is the *sacramentum fidei* and requires unqualified faith by those who receive it.'

How helpful is the ARCIC statement? It is much stronger on negative statements than it is on the positive. It bears the signs of a sincere and anguished attempt to make a statement on the Eucharistic Real Presence which will satisfy Anglicans and Roman Catholics. But it is necessarily ambiguous and open to a variety of interpretations. It must certainly be seen as such not only by Anglicans and Methodists, but by Roman Catholics too. To attempt to justify or repudiate intercommunion on the basis of a precise theological statement which is, *ipso facto*, an impossibility, is to shut the door to a shared understanding of the Eucharist which eventually Christians are unlikely to achieve until they learn to receive 'mutual correction in Christ' by experiencing the sacrament together. To insist on the 'assent of unqualified faith' from those who wish to celebrate the Eucharist together is to demand an impossible thing. Is it not characteristic of the activity of the risk-taking God that he should allow men and women in the Church to approach him even when their understanding of him and faith in him is partial, uncertain and subject to error simply because we are all human beings, creatures of time and space?

This is what Bishop Oliver Tomkins had in mind when he made his plea for intercommunion based not on theological doctrine (though he is an acknowledged expert in such matters) but on the growing recognition of Christians of many separate traditions that God is calling them at this time in our history to have the courage to move closer into unity:

> Could it be that we have not yet sufficiently appreciated the quantum leap involved in moving 'from co-operation into commitment'? Does not being Pilgrims Together draw the sting of schism and transform our presuppositions? Could not questions about the validity of sacraments, including orders, require different answers within the new relationship? Catholics are now wholly part of the process in a way which was not true when the ecumenical movement first began tentatively to raise such questions seventy or eighty years ago. The Lord who challenged us then challenges us still.[12]

Some correspondents linked their concern for open communion with their work in education and the aims of the decade of evangelism. A sister in a convent in Gloucester saw the possibility of the Eucharist playing a major role in evangelism. She felt that the Eucharist is taking a back seat because there is no way of inviting everyone to share in it. In consequence, many different forms of ecumenical worship are developed, but the Eucharist is ignored.

> I feel that all my educational efforts are falling apart at the centre. There is no way of teaching ecumenical awareness, it has to be experienced. How are we embarking on our decade of evangelism? What are we to do with our children looking for a Christ-centred way of life? We should be getting together with all Christians, and we cannot do this if we leave Eucharist worship on the sidelines. They will discover the Christ of the Eucharist if only we allow them.

Most Christians find in the Eucharist the way *par excellence* in which they can worship God in Christ and experience his creative and redemptive work. Whether or not they are able to experience this together at the Lord's Table is not a mere item on the ecumenical agenda not to be raised until it is more convenient or comfortable to do so. It is central to our hopes for unity in Christ. Those who are already able to share in the Eucharist discover a deep sense of joy and encouragement. Those who find themselves separated at the altar know that it is a grave scandal and a source of painful disappointment. As the correspondence mentioned above made abundantly clear there are no snap answers. A gulf divides those who see intercommunion as only possible when those who partake in it can express a genuinely shared conviction of the faith essential to Christian life and the order necessary for the life of the Church. For them, to 'cry Peace, Peace where there is no peace' is to indulge in ecclesiastical play-acting or dishonest wishful thinking. Those who take the traditional view of evangelical Protestantism insist that the invitation to share in the Eucharist is from the Lord himself who welcomes with open arms all who believe in him. It is not for one set of followers of Christ to deny the sacrament to others whose discipleship is no less genuine.

Both these views have risks. The 'strict' view leads to the danger of a church 'one-up-manship' which not only seems to deny the work of Christ in other people's sacramental experience, but also prevents those who hold this view from receiving 'correction from one another in Christ' which might be at its most powerful at the communion table itself. The 'lax' view which desires to open the communion table to all and sundry, leaving the response to the individual conscience with no questions asked, risks the danger of encouraging an almost casual approach to the sacrament and an individualism which is destructive of the profounder fellowship into which Christians are called.

Is there a possible compromise between these two views? Have the British Churches now reached the stage in their relations with one another when they can dare the risk of the 'quantum leap' which Bishop Oliver Tomkins advocates? This question becomes particularly urgent in ecumenical conferences and meetings in which Catholics are now taking an equal and sometimes a greater share than non-Catholics. The experience of doing so much together in the name of Christ makes it all the more painful that they must go their separate ways at the communion table. Dom Aldhelm Cameron-Brown, the Abbot of Prinknash, has said that he would welcome a 'generous allowance of intercommunion for special occasions' but feared that if it were to become general we might lose sight of our ecumenical goal.[13] It is a moot point to decide which policy will spur divided Christians to work towards real unity – the joy of sharing together in Holy Communion or the pain of recognising that we have not yet reached the point where it is honest to do so.

This is a nagging sore in the body of the Church. No quantity of magisterial or synodical resolutions or decrees will bring immediate healing. No deliberate breaking of canon law or Church discipline will bring magical solutions. Every attempt at developing a policy will bring its own risks because every answer we can give will be partially true and partially false. This is why we must at the same time be prepared in our divided state to respect one another and take risks with one another. This is why we must be prepared to be mistaken and make mistakes, because it is only by making mistakes that we shall be able to move forward. In our dialogue with one another we must learn how to be more honest, less defensive, more courageous, less ready to score points. God has taken the risk of calling men and women to belong to him through membership of his hazardous body the Church. At the heart of the Church the Eucharist is celebrated. Risk-taking is at the heart of what it means to be a member of the Church. There is no avoidance of risk, either in our understanding or practice of the sacramental mystery of our encounter with him as we eat some bread and sip some wine and dare to call it the body and blood of Christ.

INTER-FAITH

It is well known that Queen Elizabeth II places high value on her role as head of the Commonwealth. Photographs show her at her happiest and most relaxed when she is surrounded by people from her Commonwealth countries. The annual

Commonwealth Day celebration in Westminster Abbey is an event which clearly gives her special pleasure. Following the 1990 observance she was presented with a petition with 77,000 signatures protesting at the participation of non-Christian faiths alongside leaders from the Church of Scotland, Roman Catholic, Free Church and Anglicans. At this celebration it has been customary for readings to be given from the sacred texts of the Buddhists, Hindus, Muslims, Sikhs and Jews, as well as from the New Testament. The organisers of the petition wished to show no disrespect to Her Majesty, but they believed that the worship of non-Christian deities marginalised Jesus by putting him on a level with them. Tens of thousands of Christians, they said, were deeply upset by the decision of the Queen to attend an observance which was 'not compatible with the coronation oath to uphold the Protestant reformed religion established by law'. It would confirm people of other faiths in their opinion that Jesus was merely a prophet. The fact that in the following year (1991) the Queen decided not only to attend herself but chose to be accompanied by the Prince of Wales, the future head of the Commonwealth, suggests that the Queen wished to give the petition short shrift.

The question of the relationship of the Christian religion with other faiths is one of increasing urgency. Some ecumenical enthusiasts wish to include other religions within their area of concern. The place of multi-faith education in the schools' religious studies syllabus is of growing relevance, especially where there are large ethnic minority populations. The decade of evangelism is seen by the adherents of other world faiths as a threat and by some Christian evangelists as an opportunity.

The hymns of Reginald Heber are still sung in some churches. He was made Bishop of Calcutta in 1823 at a time of great imperial expansion in the wake of which missionaries were carrying the Bible, the Book of Common Prayer and the western way of life to India, Africa, Java, and Greenland's icy mountains, as Bishop Heber sang:

> From many an ancient river,
> From many a palmy plain,
> They call us to deliver
> Their land from error's chain . . .

In vain with lavish kindness
The gifts of God are strown;
The heathen in his blindness
Bows down to wood and stone.

It was initially a 'take it or leave it' form of evangelism which those missionaries with great courage employed. But they had a narrow view. Everyone who was not a Christian was a heathen. The task of mission was to smash idols and replace pagan superstition with the Good News. Now the descendants of those 'heathen' who lived in what were once called the 'mission fields' have come to live as our neighbours in many parts of multi-faith Britain. Some of them, in their turn, now see us as bowing down to idols, not of wood and stone but (perhaps worse) the idols of materialism, monetarism, sexual satisfaction, addiction, greed, pornography and a desperate search for higher living standards. Some see pagan Britain as their mission field. There are now as many Muslims in Britain as there are Methodists. Some young people search for a spirituality in certain forms of eastern mysticism which they cannot find in western Christianity. This poses a problem for the decade of evangelism which is not easy to solve.

The World Wide Fund for Nature organised in the autumn of 1989 a Festival of Faith and the Environment. It took place in and around Canterbury Cathedral. It opened with the arrival in the city of three pilgrim groups led by Anglican, Baha'i and Hindu ministers of religion. There were exhibitions and displays mounted in the vicinity of the cathedral by members of environmental groups and different faiths. The Archbishop (Runcie) preached at the Sunday morning Eucharist. Protests were orchestrated from the same sources which opposed the Westminster Abbey celebration, though there was no multi-faith worship in the cathedral. In his sermon the Archbishop carefully argued the theological treatment of 'green issues' both biblically and scientifically. 'The new interest in ecology and the environment', he said, 'is the stirring of a human concern which can genuinely be called "religious". The Christian faith, and some other religions too, can welcome this movement as following from a belief in a Creator of the universe.'[14] But the critics were not satisfied. The Revd Tony Higton saw in such an event the perils of worshipping 'other gods and idols, earth worship, inter-faith worship, occult practices from mediums and the like, recruiting campaigns for other religions, sects and cults'. Dr David Samuel of the Church Society was less sensational but regretted that the brochure advertising the Festival implied a 'parity of religions and a mingling of beliefs'. He also noted that Christians were mentioned after Buddhists and Muslims in the list of religions involved in the Festival.

Those who pursue the path of inter-faith dialogue and worship remain unconvinced by the 'hard line' approach. It was the specific wish of Pope John XXIII that the Second Vatican Council should make a statement on the status and value of other world religions. The statement *Nostra Aetate* declared that the Church 'rejects nothing which is true and holy in these religions'. It began with a statement about humanity's common religious quest and ended with a strong repudiation of any discrimination on the basis of race, colour, religion or condition of life as foreign to the mind of Christ. The Roman Catholic bishops of England and Wales referred to this Vatican II declaration in their response to the 1980 Pastoral Congress. The Council, they pointed out, urged Catholics to look on the other great world religions with respect and recognise that God is also in them:

> The Church now encourages us to approach them in a spirit of dialogue, of listening and sharing with humility. This has had an enormous significance for overseas mission. But the time has come for us to absorb its lesson for our own situation at home. We are now part of a society which is multi-cultural and multi-religious. So far, in England and Wales, our official contacts and consultations with non-Christian religions have been limited to our valued link with the Jewish faith. We should try to become much better acquainted with the background and beliefs of non-Christian immigrants to our countries. In particular we should approach them in a spirit of openness and humility, to learn, to understand, to appreciate and gain from their religious traditions. At the same time we should make

known to them our own belief, the good news of Jesus Christ.[15]

There are voices in the Church of England which echo this same theme. A report from the General Synod's Board for Mission and Unity states:

> As the Christian and non-Christian enter ever deeper into a relationship of profound mutual respect, there is the possibility of catching fresh glimpses of the one eternal God. Dialogue in this sense is more than communication; it may become communion in which we are mutually informed, illumined and re-united to ourselves, to one another and to God.[16]

Dr Max Warren, the much-respected missionary thinker, always insisted that the gospel could not be commended to people of other faiths unless they were first met in the spirit of Christian love, humility and a readiness to learn. Both Jews and Arabs have good reason to distrust Christians. Anti-semitism is a Christian disease with its roots in the New Testament story. Jewish people will never forget the scars of the holocaust which was perpetrated by a country which claimed to be Christian. The Muslims do not forget the Crusades and the cruelty shown against Islam by European warriors wearing the symbol of the cross of Christ on their armour. Saddam Hussein's language during the Gulf war, declaring himself to be fighting a *jihad*, a holy war against the infidel and the forces of Satan, was an attempt to resurrect the spirit of the Crusades when Christians waged a holy war against the followers of the Prophet and used exactly the same kind of language to encourage their troops. If for no other reason, Christians have the opportunity now of redeeming the past in acts of friendship and respect for Jews and Muslims and those of other faiths who have good reason to be suspicious of the followers of Jesus Christ.

On the first two Sunday evenings after the start of the land battle in the Gulf war, the BBC broadcast special transmissions of *Songs of Praise* from Westminster Abbey and Dunblane Cathedral in Scotland. On each occasion prayers were led by Jewish, Muslim and Christian ministers. The involvement in the Middle East conflict of the three great monotheistic world religions, Christianity, Judaism and Islam, gave many people food for thought on the inter-faith situation, and their involvement in two impressive acts of worship, witnessed nationwide on television, was entirely appropriate.

The Roman Catholic theologian Hans Küng has in recent years made a special study of Christianity and its relationship to other world religions. He has given his conclusions in the light of the Gulf war:

> Jews, Christians and Muslims believe in one God who tolerates no other gods, powers, rulers and figures beside himself; who is not just the God of one people but of all peoples, not a national God but Lord of the world, who wants the well-being of all peoples.
>
> Jews, Christians and Muslims hold fast to a basic prophetic ethic: humane demands for justice, truth, faithfulness, peace and love – which are claimed as requirements of God himself.
>
> Judaism, Christianity and Islam have been shaped by the prophetic criticism of the unjust and inhuman conditions under which humiliated, enslaved and exploited people have to live – there can be no worship of God without respect of human beings and human rights.

This leads Küng to ask whether on the basis of the Hebrew Bible, the New Testament and the Koran, could not Jews and Muslims, together with Christians, work together on the problems of the Middle East which so profoundly concern them all? And he adds:

> No one should say that this is impossible. Fifty years ago individual small groups began dialogue between Catholics and Protestants: they were told that this made no sense. Today the situation between the Christian professions, which earlier were at total enmity in a way that led to numerous wars, hot and cold, has changed: they accept one another even if they have not yet lifted all the mutual excommunications.[17]

Archbishop Runcie has spoken of the discoveries which can

be made through inter-faith dialogue if it is carried on in the
right spirit:

> Through nurturing a spirit of friendship and reconciliation
> true dialogue can help to overcome religious divisiveness
> and create new conditions for greater fellowship and deeper
> communion. It can help us to recognise that other faiths
> than our own are genuine mansions of the Spirit with many
> rooms to be discovered rather than solitary fortresses to be
> attacked.

Christianity is, in origin, a Middle East religion. As it spread
into Europe it became strongly influenced by the thought and
outlook of the Graeco-Roman world, and later it became strongly influenced by the western culture which it also helped to
form. Estranged from its roots, the Church has found it difficult
to proclaim its faith in the language and thought appropriate
for the part of the world from which it originally sprang. The
Jewish people can help us to understand the Jewishness of the
Old Testament, of Jesus and the first Christian communities.
Muslims may help us towards a better appreciation of the
common heritage from which both our faiths were born. But
this can only be achieved in an atmosphere of respect, humility
and the kind of honest dialogue which leads to the mutual
trust and friendship in which Christ may be truly commended.
Christians can embark on contacts of this sort with adherents
of other faiths without disloyalty to their own beliefs. As Bishop
David Sheppard told his diocesan synod when they were beginning to discuss the decade of evangelism:

> I do not believe that respect for the other person means
> that we should avoid speaking of our own faith. True
> respect will mean sharing the most precious things of our
> faith if there comes an opportune moment. It will also
> include opening ourselves to want to listen to the precious
> things of the other's faith. I believe such dialogue to be the
> appropriate approach to members of other living faiths.

Such dialogue is full of risks, as opponents are quick to point
out. The uniqueness of God's revelation in Christ may be
blurred and distorted. But to attempt, as best we may, to share

in honest dialogue and humble prayer alongside those whose faith in God takes them along different paths from ourselves is a risk well worth taking. For it may lead us to discover that God has correction to bring to us from unexpected sources, and to experience new visions of Christ's kind of loving which breaks down barriers, removes suspicions and old hostilities and breathes the spirit of reconciliation.

Such an attitude of mind and heart may not only help to widen our own narrow horizons: it may enable us to make some contribution, however small, to peace and understanding in our sadly divided world.

UNSETTLED OUTLOOK

JESUS ONCE TOLD a story about an entrepreneur who, having to make an extended trip abroad, left some of his employees to carry on the business in his absence.[1] They were talented men, so he felt able to trust them to make their own judgements on how the finances of the enterprises might be improved in his absence. In due course he would return and see what progress they had been able to make. Two of the men managed to make good use of the capital entrusted to them and were able to show a handsome profit when the boss returned. A third was less successful because he had been less adventurous. He was nervous that his investment policy might fail. He dared not take risks. He thought it wise to keep his share of the capital intact. If he could not show a profit, at least he would avoid the danger of making a loss. On his return home the owner of the business was intensely displeased. The unsuccessful investor was summarily dismissed. Those who had taken risks, and succeeded, were handsomely rewarded. Commenting on this story C. H. Dodd[2] remarks how the central focus of the parable is not on the two successful workers, but 'on the scrupulous servant who would take no risks'. This man is blamed, not only for his excessive caution but because he was in breach of the trust which his boss had put on him. What sort of person had Jesus in mind when he painted this picture? Dodd answers that it is an attack on the Pharisees who sought personal security by a meticulous observance of the Law. It was precisely the risk that the early Christians took, and they took it under the inspiration of their Master. It is this kind of risk that all investment of capital involves; without the risk of investment the capital remains barren.

It is worth noting that the employer is also a risk-taker. His employees have worked with him and they understand his mind and his methods. On the strength of this, he is ready to take the risk of entrusting the business to them with its precious assets. He does not appear to have left them with detailed instructions. He relies on their knowledge, experience and common sense. He does not keep coming back to see how they are getting on. He does not fuss over them. He is even prepared for one or other of them to make a mess of the job. This story is of great encouragement to those many Christians who do not feel that they have immediate and direct access to divine guidance at all times through some heavenly telex machine. They know that God has revealed his nature to them through the Bible, through the created universe, through the unfolding story of the Church, through their reason, conscience and ordinary common sense. They know that he has entrusted them with this rich heritage, and that he leaves them with the job of doing the best they can in working for the coming of the kingdom on earth. They do not see him as an interfering God. He does not fuss over them. He takes the great risk, which is the risk of love, of treating them as responsible adults. He knows that they will make mistakes, with many false starts and many failures. Yet he trusts them to be trustworthy. They believe that he watches over their activities with the amalgam of judgement and mercy to which Scripture constantly bears witness. They know that in some way (how, they cannot understand) there will be a reckoning. In the meantime they are convinced that even if at times he seems to have gone away to a distant country, such is the nature of his love that he has promised that his Spirit will never leave them: At the same time that he totally respects their independence and freedom, there is always the assurance that 'underneath are the everlasting arms'. So this parable is, *par excellence*, the story of a risk-taking God.

The men in the parable, entrusted precariously with their master's rich capital, reflect the Church to which, after his resurrection, Jesus took the risk of entrusting the good news of God whom he had made known through his life and teaching, death and rising to new life. Anyone who reads an honest account of the story of the Church during the first two thousand years of its existence, or who examines its life and work in the world today, cannot be left with any doubt that here, in stark clarity, is seen the evidence of the risk-taking nature of the God whom we dare to call love. Those who lead pilgrimage parties to the Holy Land, can never fail to be embarrassed by a visit to the Church of the Holy Sepulchre in Jerusalem, arguably the most sacred spot in Christendom. 'Anyone hoping to find harmony and quiet contemplation reigning among the Christian communities in that famous church', comments the Baedeker guide book 'is due for a disappointment – the sects are on a Cold War footing.' This experience led Rose Macaulay in *The Towers of Trebizond* to put into the mouth of her heroine a brilliant 'potted history' of the Church which

> grew so far, almost at once, from anything which can have been intended, and became so blood-stained and persecuting and cruel and war-like and made small and trivial things so important, and tried to exclude everything not done in a certain way and by certain people, and stamped out heresies with such cruelty and rage. And this failure of the Christian Church, of every branch of it in every country, is one of the saddest things that has happened in all the world. But it is what happens when a magnificent idea has to be worked out by human beings who do not understand much of it but interpret it in their own way and think they are guided by God, who they have not yet grasped. And yet they had grasped something, so that the Church has always had great magnificence and much courage, and people have died for it in agony, which is supposed to balance all the other people who have had to die in agony because they did not accept it, and it has flowered up in learning and culture and beauty and art, to set against its darkness and incivility and obscurantism and barbarity and nonsense, and it has produced saints and martyrs and kindness and goodness, though these have also occurred freely outside it, and it is a wonderful and most extraordinary pageant of contradictions, and I, at least, want to be inside it, though it is foolishness to most of my friends.[3]

It is worth recalling that Dame Rose Macaulay wrote those stunning words when she had recently returned from a period of estrangement, back to her beloved Anglican Church of which she was a devoted member. This is a refreshingly honest picture of the Church of yesterday and today. Who would be bold enough to say that it might not be equally true of the Church of the future? Who can tell? About the immediate future, it can be said with certainty that God will continue to take risks with his Church, and his Church will continue to take risks with its God.

This final chapter is being written during the week in which Dr George Leonard Carey was enthroned in the chair of St Augustine to be the 103rd Archbishop of Canterbury. For a brief spell the Church of England is hitting headlines with material devoid of scandal. The ancient ecclesiastical ceremony in Canterbury Cathedral makes good television viewing. The inclusion of a little modest religious 'pop music' adds a new and harmless touch of spice to the occasion. The new archbishop appears before the public as a refreshing personality, proud of his comparatively humble origins, and radiating a kind of gospel optimism with his readiness to join in cheerful evangelical sing-alongs with clap-happy evangelicals with whom he obviously feels at home. He shares something of the popular charisma of Pope John Paul II who had no difficulty in stimulating 4,000 non-Catholics to applaud him to the rooftops when he entered Liverpool Anglican Cathedral in 1982 in the course of the papal visit to England. But there the resemblance ends. Pope John Paul sees as his mission the task of recalling his Church to the old basic certainties of yesterday. The promise of George Carey is that he will have the courage to lead his people into a new understanding of Christ and his gospel by courageously following the uncertainties of tomorrow.

The new man at Lambeth comes from a different mould from his immediate predecessors in office – Michael Ramsey, Donald Coggan and Robert Runcie – though he is closer to Coggan than he is to the other two. He is labelled an evangelical, and is proud of that particular heritage. Yet when he became Bishop of Bath and Wells in 1987 he was determined not be be stereotyped as a party man. He led a diocesan pilgrimage to the shrine of Our Lady of Walsingham – not a typical evangelical activity! He was concerned to make known his sympathies across a broad ecclesiastical spectrum. He informed the press that although he did not deny an evangelical influence, he was concerned not to be labelled an evangelical archbishop. He said, 'I am an Anglican bishop. Over the years I have gained a lot from catholic spirituality, from liberal studies of the Bible, from the charismatic renewal movement. I will not deny what shaped me. But I want to affirm that I am an Anglican first and foremost.'

A few months before his enthronement the archbishop-elect gave an interview to *Reader's Digest*. It attracted most attention for his comments on the ordination of women. But it included a description of the Church of England which verged on caricature and must have caused some offence to the large number of elderly women (and men) whose steadfast loyalty in many parishes has prevented (or postponed) the closing of their local church many years ago. He described the Church as 'an elderly lady who mutters away to herself in a corner, ignored most of the time'. The greatest challenge facing the Church, he said, was to 'present the Christian faith simply, so that people can understand and follow it'. But if this 'granny' is to be so obsessed with quarrelling about the family inheritance with her other elderly relatives, grumbling toothlessly about their 'heresy' and suchlike, she will be ignored.

That picture has some truth in it, but it is over-pessimistic. Although statistical returns give little evidence of any significant increase in the number of people attending worship with regularity, experience bears out Dr John Habgood's assertion from his subjective assessment from visiting parishes that 'there are a great many lively and forward-looking churches in sharp contrast to the gloomy prognostications often made about the Church of England by the media.' On the day of Dr Carey's enthronement, Richard Harries, the Bishop of Oxford, wrote in *The Times* about the spirit of cautious optimism that many people claimed to detect among the Christian Churches in England in the spring of 1991. He thought that there was a strong sense of being in business again. 'Under Dr Runcie's intelligent, humane and distinguished leadership, the Church of England slogged through difficult times, and emerged as a force to be reckoned with. Dr Carey, with his quick mind, willingness to learn and spiritual robustness, is the right man to take the Church on a quick march forward.'[4]

But no amount of ecclesiastical euphoria must be allowed to disguise the fact that if the Church is to be true to its mission, it must expect tough times ahead as it has faced them in the past. When Dr Runcie announced his resignation there was much idle talk expressing the hope that a new archbishop would be a sort of vacuum cleaner, tidying up the mess left by the permissive and 'liberal' years of the 1960s and 1970s – 'the legacy of unresolved problems and old conflicts', as the *Observer* writer quoted earlier put it. People were feeling that at last the Church could return to a 'normal Christianity' – as if there could ever be such a state as normality in a dynamic faith. When Dr Carey finally leaves office, he, too, will leave behind him 'unresolved problems and old conflicts' – as will all the other archbishops who follow after him.

In recent years the charismatic movement has been in the ascendant and liberalism in the Church has suffered a decline. But the situation will change – and then change again. Throughout the history of the Church the charismatic movement has appeared, disappeared and then appeared again. This is how it should be. When it comes, it serves to provide a dull Church with a much-needed booster dose of enthusiasm. If it remains for too long, it weakens the Christian body by feeding it with too much junk food. In the same way liberalism comes and goes in spells, rescuing the Church from mental paralysis with a much-needed stimulus to mind and imagination, but an overdose can loosen valuable foundations. Meanwhile middle-of-the-road Christians continue their traditional worship at a fairly steady pace, not much affected by the influences from either side. Such influences, coming and going, will persist, varying from time to time in strength and impact. This is part of the necessary dynamic of a living Church. They only become dangerous if adherents to one 'movement' or another begin to claim that they have found the exclusive key to the truth. Pluralism is to be valued, as Dr Carey said in his enthronement sermon.

In our own time there are other challenges which will test us deeply – not only the ordination of women but also the challenge to live with and accept gratefully the diverse traditions which make up the breadth of Anglicanism . . . Members of the Church must put witness to God above their divisions. We shall only be able to do that if we stand together even when decisions are made which cause us terrible pain.

There are hard questions to be faced about the meaning and strategy of evangelism in this closing decade of the twentieth century. Archbishop Carey has said that the greatest challenge facing the Church is to 'present the Christian faith simply so that people can understand it and follow it'. But a 'health warning' has to be attached to statements of that kind – true though they may be. Of course the gospel can be understood and accepted with the deepest significance in the hearts and minds of the simplest followers of Christ. Their devotion can often shame the sophistication of those who claim to approach the gospel more intellectually. But in evangelism, as in all religious communication, a clear distinction must be made between simplicity and simplism. John Harriott, quoted in the opening chapter, speaking about the vast mysteries of our faith, rightly warned that the evangelist who reduces them to a few lines which might come off a cornflakes packet is dealing with cartoons and not masterpieces, sowing cynicism and despair rather than faith. It is better, he said, for people to shrink from the gospel because it is too great than because it is too small. Whilst some will be attracted temporarily by the slick slogans and pop songs of popular evangelism, many more will be repelled by their superficiality. An urgent task, and a risky one, is to find ways of presenting the gospel which engage at a serious level the critical intelligence and contemporary imagination of men and women nurtured in the science, politics and culture of today. As Harriot said, these people will not (or should not) be converted by Mickey Mouse Christianity. C. S. Lewis once said, 'We need two sorts of evangelists: evangelists for the head and evangelists for the heart. We have long been short of the first kind.'[5] This is a task to which the Churches have been sadly slow to address themselves.

The closing months of 1990 and the beginning of 1991 have been dubbed 'the ecumenical winter with the new growth waiting underground'. The end of the British Council of Churches in the spring of 1990 was marked by an impressive act of worship of thanksgiving for the past and dedication for the future. Representatives from many different Christian traditions took part. The final act was a procession from the hall where the service had taken place out into the gardens of the Swanwick Conference Centre. Each one moved out singing a hymn and carrying a lighted candle to receive a final blessing from the Archbishop of Canterbury. At a crucial moment the wind blew, and many of the candles were extinguished. One delegate was heard to say to another as his candle flame was blown out, 'I wonder if this is a symbol of the future of the ecumenical movement in Britain.'

At Dr Carey's enthronement many Churches were represented by a phalanx of dignitaries. When the time came for communion many of them were not able to share in the sacrament together. Dr Carey frankly acknowledged this fact as he welcomed them. 'Your presence is evidence of that slow but steady movement towards greater unity which has been one of the most remarkable gifts of God to us in these times. And yet there remains a sadness at the heart of today's ceremony.' If the ecumenical movement is to make significant progress in the coming years, it will not do so unless the Churches are prepared to take great risks for the sake of unity. Will the Church of England, and especially its clergy, continue to put obstacles in the way of every imaginative and hard-thought scheme presented to them? Will the welcome participation of the Roman Catholic Church in the ecumenical process make it even less likely that risks will be taken? The ecumenical movement in Britain faces a difficult time ahead. Progress will not be easy. Progress without risk will be impossible.

In the opinion of Robert Runcie's biographer, the Archbishop's Commission Report on Urban Priority Areas, *Faith in the City*, is likely to stand as the greatest single achievement of his primacy. It was also the occasion which brought him into sharpest conflict with the more right wing members of Margaret Thatcher's government. Those who saw this as indicative of the prophetic role which the Church must take in the modern secular state were relieved to know that Runcie's successor had launched, when in his former diocese, a broadside against the poll tax. Dr Carey took pains to emphasise this point in his enthronement sermon. 'No Church', he said, 'should avoid political comment when freedom, dignity and worth are threatened.' Evangelism is usually seen as a call to the individual to personal repentance and commitment. That must have a key place in the proclamation of the gospel. But it is not the whole story. The lives of individuals are profoundly influenced by the political, economic, social and industrial structures which society creates and tolerates. The great Old Testament prophets addressed their evangelistic message not only to individuals but equally to communities and nations. The decade of evangelism must make clear to all who will listen that the gospel of Jesus Christ challenges the values by which people are governed, and the presuppositions by which society organises itself. If the Church is to fulfil its prophetic task in the coming decade it must be ready to risk the same political conflicts which characterised the Thatcher years.

Demands are always being made of Church leaders that they should give clear moral guidance on the problems of today. People expect precise answers to emerge from some divine computer when the correct keys are pressed. The complex moral problems facing society, many of them unknown to previous generations, cannot be precisely answered by quotations from the Ten Commandments, the Sermon on the Mount or random Bible texts. Jesus left great moral principles to provide the raw materials for making moral judgements. He did not leave detailed instructions, nor can detailed answers be expected to fall down from heaven as if from a Delphic oracle. This is why there is not a major moral problem upon which Christians of equal intelligence and spirituality do not find themselves in disagreement. This is why there is no clearly unanimous Christian opinion on such matters as contraception, divorce, homosexual relations, genetic engineering, transplant surgery, censorship and other aspects of the human sciences, even more complex, on which decisions have to be made. Snap judgements, petitions, protest marches are generally frivolous ways of coming to moral judgements without any serious engagement on the technical and theological issues involved. The Church cannot dodge such issues. It must make its voice heard in the public debate. But it must avoid pontificating simply on the basis of emotional response, ignorance, gut reaction or the mindless sway of pressure group propaganda. To enter this field is a risky business. It can lead to much misunderstanding. But to refuse to face these issues would be a dereliction of Christian duty.

None of these questions, theological, ecclesiastical, ethical or personal can be solved satisfactorily by digging up ancient shibboleths or quoting old texts. They call for exploration, not dogmatism. God is on the move and we must learn to move with him. Dr George Macleod once described idolatry as essentially the worship of a static God. In *Coracle*, the magazine of the Iona Community which he founded, he gave expression to this faith. 'Christ is a person to be trusted, not a principle to be tested. The Church is a Movement, not a meeting house. The Faith is an experience, not an exposition. Christians are Explorers, not map makers.'[6] So the risk-taking God invites us to look forward with courage to the future rather than cling fearfully to the past. This is a precarious invitation, fraught with danger. But it is not playing safe which is creative; it is daring to move ahead, leaving the past behind. Karl Rahner gave this advice to his fellow priests in the Roman Catholic Church in Germany.

> It seems to me that the courage to abandon positions no longer tenable means asking modestly, but realistically and insistently, whether it is always possible to take with us on this march to the Church's future all the fine fellows whose out of date mentality is opposed to a march into the unknown future. For if we enter on it, we shall be able to keep in the Church, or in friendly relations with it, not a few who are in any case on the way to the future; but we shall also estrange, shock and scandalise not a few who feel at home only in the Church as they have been accustomed to it in the past. Certainly we must modestly and charitably show consideration to these 'conservatives' as far as this is at all possible, but there is no Christian principle to the effect that the conservatives must always be in the right when a choice has to be made between the two groups.[7]

Christians do not generally find it hard to agree about the generalities of their faith. But once they move from vague dogmatic principles and pious utterances and get down to the deeper theological and ethical questions, they find wide differences of interpretations amongst Christians of equal intelligence and equal devotion to Jesus Christ as Lord and Saviour. How could it be otherwise? We creatures trapped in the time-space dimension reach out to God who, as John of Damascus put it, is infinite and incomprehensible. Ultimately all we can know about him is his infinity and incomprehensibility. So we need the humility and the good sense to know that all our theological statements and ethical judgements must have about them an element of provisionality. That is why we desperately need to hear one another and help one another so that together we may travel towards a growing understanding of truth and goodness even though final solutions elude us.

And this is why we must not be frightened of the kind of confrontation which in practice inevitably leads to compromise. Such compromise can significantly take us forward if our talking together is not conducted in a spirit of proud competition or clever point-scoring, but is surrounded and made secure by that love and trust which Christians are supposed to show to one another. Love and trust alone can make possible total honesty with one another and total openness to one another. This is not to fudge issues: it is to face up to the truth as best we may.

Here is a major task before all the Churches and at every level as we move towards the huge challenges of the next century. It is a major task in our synods, clergy fraternals, local ecumenical parishes and projects, and in Councils of Churches. But equally important is the involvement of women and men in the congregations, no longer hiding from them the real questions which the modern world poses to their faith – questions which are often discussed on radio and television with greater honesty than in the Churches. This means clearing away some of the trivialities of Church life which seem often to be used simply as ways of protecting laity from the huge theological and ethical issues which are every bit as much their concern as they are of the clergy and the theologians.

Only by such a passion for truth and such a capacity for honesty will the Churches be able to offer what people really must have as they try to puzzle out what this Christian business means out there in the increasingly secular and materialistic world. They must not continue to be offered a diminishingly effective protection from that world in the closed mentality of a pious inward-looking ghetto.

This can be very disturbing to some people as they discover that faith is not simply the acceptance of a set-piece formula based on often unclear passages of Scripture, or on creeds and prescriptions of venerable ecclesiastical institutions of long ago. Faith is an exciting, risky and challenging exploration into the truth about God. It is risky to let go some of the past in order to be liberated for the future. But the evidence of the way that God has worked in the Bible, and in the Church and in the work of creation as revealed by modern physics and biology, is a sure sign that the God with whom we have to do is a risk-taking God. When in the exploration of our faith and the working out of that faith in practice, we find ourselves travelling into risky territory, we know that this is because we are made in his risk-taking image.

The Church of the future will certainly make as many mistakes as it has in the past. But the greatest mistake it could possibly make would be to be too frightened to take any more risks at all.

NOTES

CHAPTER 1   PRESENT INDICATIVES

1   Adrian Hastings, *Robert Runcie* (Mowbray 1991).
2   John Harriott, *The Tablet*, 4 August 1990.
3   'You have seven seconds', *The Tablet*, 18 August 1990.
4   Karl Rahner, *The Shape of the Church to Come* (SPCK 1974).

CHAPTER 2   BIBLE

1   Genesis 6:5–7.
2   Genesis 9:18–24.
3   Gordon Mursell, *Out of the Deep* (DLT 1989). See particularly pp. 42–60.
4   Philippians 3:13.
5   Luke 1:1.
6   Matthew 4:1–11.
7   John 4:1–42.
8   Luke 13:32.
9   Matthew 23:27.

CHAPTER 3   CREATION

1   Wisdom 7:16–21.
2   For a fuller and very readable account of the Darwin controversy see Owen Chadwick, *The Victorian Church* vol. 1 (A. and C. Black 1970).
3   Romans 8:22–24.
4   C. E. Raven, *Christ and the Modern Opportunity* (SCM Press 1956).
5   Pierre Teilhard de Chardin, *The Phenomenon of Man* (Collins 1959), p. 297.

6   John Polkinghorne, *One World* (SPCK 1986), p. 60.
7   For further reading: Stephen Hawking, *A Brief History of Time* (Bantam Press 1988). The publishers of this remarkable best-seller claim that it makes modern space-time theory accessible and clear for the general reader. Those not trained in scientific discipline may find some of the passages difficult to follow. But perseverance is rewarded by a breath-taking vision of the origins of our universe.
8   John Polkinghorne, *Science and Creation*, (SPCK 1988), p. 60. Dr Polkinghorne's two books mentioned in these notes, together with *Science and Providence* (SPCK 1989), provide a valuable introduction to the study of the interaction between science and theology.
9   *Science and Creation*, p. 48.
10 Arthur Peacocke, *God and the New Biology* (Dent 1986), p 62. Dr Peacocke's book discusses the same issues as in the writings of Dr Polkinghorne, but from the point of view of a biologist who is also a theologian.
11 David Attenborough, *Life on Earth* (Collins/BBC 1979), p. 308.
12 David Jenkins, *God, Miracle, and the Church of England* (SCM Press 1988).
13 *One World*, p. 69.

CHAPTER 4   CREED

1   John Robinson, *Honest to God* (SCM Press 1963). For further reading on the *Honest to God* debate see: Mervyn Stockwood, *Chanctonbury Ring* (Hodder and Stoughton (1982). Eric James, *The Life of Bishop John Robinson* (Collins 1987).
2   *Honest to God*, p. 18.
3   *The Nature of Christian Belief*, a statement and exposition by the House of Bishops of the General Synod of the Church of England (Church House Publishing 1986).
4   ibid., pp. 6, 7.
5   ibid., p. 9.
6   Hans Küng, *Infallibility? An Enquiry*, (Collins), p. 138. This was first published in 1971 and has recently been re-issued in an updated edition.
7   Philippians 1:9.
8   Rahner, *The Shape of the Church to Come*, p. 38.
9   *The Times*, 10 April 1985.
10 Hans Küng, *On Being a Christian* (Collins 1976), p. 343.

CHAPTER 5 AUTHORITY

1 The Anglican-Roman Catholic International Commission (ARCIC), *The Final Report* (SPCK/CTS), p. 52.
2 Rahner, *The Shape of the Church to Come*, p. 84.
3 *The Easter People*. A Message from the Roman Catholic Bishops of England and Wales in the light of the National Pastoral Congress, Liverpool 1980 (St Paul Publications 1980), p. 17.
4 ibid., p. 38.
5 ibid., p. 11.
6 ibid., p. 14.
7 Rahner, *The Shape of the Church to Come*, p. 121.
8 Graham Greene in an extensive interview in *The Tablet*, 23 September 1989.
9 *Episcopal Ministry* (The Cameron Report) from the Archbishops' Group on the Episcopate (Church House Publications 1990).
10 ibid., p. 167.
11 *The Nature of Christian Belief*, p. 36.
12 Adrian Hastings, *A History of English Christianity 1920–1985* (Collins 1986), p. 664.

CHAPTER 6 MINISTRY

1 *The Lima Report: Baptism, Eucharist and the Ministry* (Faith and Order Paper 111, World Council of Churches 1982), p. 23.
2 *Faith in the Countryside*, Report of the Archbishops' Commission on Rural Areas (Churchman Publishing 1990), p. 155.
3 *Ordained Ministry in Secular Employment* (ACCM Occasional Paper 31, February 1989).
4 Peter Baelz and William Jacob. (eds), *Ministers of the Kingdom: Exploration in Non-Stipendiary Ministry* (CIO Publishing, 1985), p. 38.
5 Rahner, *The Shape of the Church to Come*, p. 109.
6 ibid, p. 110.
7 *Faith in the City*, Report of the Archbishop of Canterbury's Commission on Urban Priority Areas (Church House Publising 1985), pp. 112ff.
8 *Episcopal Ministry*, p. 245.
9 Acts of the Apostles 5:34–39.
10 Father Brian O'Sullivan, chairman of the National Conference of Priests, writing in *The Tablet*, 29 September 1990.

CHAPTER 7   ECUMENISM

1   William Temple's enthronement sermon is printed in *The Church Looks Forward* (Macmillan 1944).
2   *Churches together in Pilgrimage* (BCC/CTS 1989).
3   Owen Chadwick, *Michael Ramsey, A Life* (Oxford 1990), pp. 333ff.
4   William Purcell, *Fisher of London* (Hodder and Stoughton 1969), p. 283.
5   *Churches Together in Pilgrimage*, p. 7.
6   ibid., Introduction.
7   David L. Edwards, *The British Churches Turn to the Future* (SCM 1973), pp. 25ff.
8   *Easter People*, p. 29.
9   ibid. p. 29.
10   Father Michael Simpson SJ, *The Tablet*, 29 September 1990.
11   ARCIC, *The Final Report*, p. 21.
12   *The Tablet*, 13 October 1990.
13   *The Tablet*, 10 November 1990.
14   Archbishop Runcie's sermon on this occasion is included in Adrian Hastings' biography.
15   *Easter People*, p. 31.
16   *The Measure of Mission* (General Synod Board for Mission and Unity 1987), p. 29.
17   *The Tablet*, 2 March 1991.

CHAPTER 8   UNSETTLED OUTLOOK

1   Matthew 25:14–30; Luke 19:12–27.
2   C. H. Dodd, *The Parables of the Kingdom* (Nisbet 1935), pp. 146ff.
3   Rose Macaulay, *The Towers of Trebizond* (Collins 1956), ch. 17.
4   *The Times*. 19 April 1991.
5   Quoted in William Abraham, *The Logic of Evangelism* (Hodder and Stoughton 1989).
6   Quoted in Ronald Ferguson, *George MacLeod* (Collins 1990).
7   Rahner, *The Shape of the Church to Come*, p. 49.